WHEREFORE*⁾ ART THOU, THIRD GENDER

A SCIENCE FICTION NOVEL PLUS A SCIENTIFIC TREATISE ON THE BIRTH AND EXISTENCE OF GAY PERSONS

By Dr. Z. Gilead

*) A paraphrase on Shakespeare's Romeo and Juliette "Oh wherefore art thou Roneo". "Wherefore" in old English meant "what are you, Romeo"," and not "where are you" as many think

Copyright © 2022 **Z. Gilead**

All rights reserved. No part of this publication may be reproduced, distributed, or transmitted in any form or by any means, including photocopying, recording, or other electronic or mechanical methods, without the prior written permission of the publisher, except in the case of brief quotations embodied in critical reviews and certain other noncommercial uses permitted by copyright law. For permission requests, write to the publisher, addressed "Attention: Book Rights and Permission," at the address below.

Published in the United States of America

ISBN 978-1-956741-94-0 (SC)

Z. Gilead
222 West 6th Street
Suite 400, San Pedro, CA, 90731
www.stellarliterary.com

Order Information and Rights Permission:

Quantity sales. Special discounts might be available on quantity purchases by corporations, associations, and others.
For details, contact the publisher at the address above.

For Book Rights Adaptation and other Rights Permission. Call us at toll-free 1-888-945-8513 or send us an email at admin@stellarliterary.com.

Contents

INTRODUCTION ii
    Chapter 1: The Scientist 1
    Chapter 2: The Professor Teaches… 8
    Chapter 3: The evangelist sponsor 10
    Chapter 4: The Scientist meet the evangelist 18
    Chapter 5: The Evangelist billionaire expresses a wish and the professor complies. 22
    Chapter 6: Population studies intended to show that DNA is the culprit ... 27
    Chapter 7: Are genes the only key factors in producing gay persons? 39
    Chapter 8: Pheromones and homosexuality 41
    Chapter 9: The Scientists of the start-up company 51
    Chapter 10: The professor describes the project of the start-up company ... 58
    Chapter 11: The wonderful Vomeronasal organ 67
    Chapter 12: Jill suggests an additional project to obtain a conversion 72
    Chapter 13: The resection of the VMO 77
    Chapter 14: The Temptation 81
    Chapter 15: Re-appraisal of phase two of the research 87
    Chapter 16: The blocking of the VMO's receptors with antibodies 90
    Chapter 17: The Genetic Correction of the Donner Fetus 96
    Chapter 18: The use of carbon nanotubes 105
    Chapter 19: "Let my people go (be)!" 112
    Chapter 20: The dissolution of the start-up company 115
    Chapter 21: Donner and Axel rejoice and thank God and the scientists ... 118
THE AUTHORS BIOGRAPHY 123

APOLOGY

I want to apologize to those of my readers who may consider my novel insulting or patronizing. I am straight man myself, but my intention was the complete reverse of 'offensive' or 'patronizing'. I bring a lot of scientific studies that show, what is a common knowledge today: A large percent of Gays and lesbian people are born this way because of genetic and hormonal influences, and their sexual orientation is not a "learned, willing depravity". However, if this novel offends anyone of my readers, I ask his/her forgiveness.

INTRODUCTION

Dear readers:

The novel that you hold in your hands is composed of two parts: **Part 1**: A Scientific essay that describes the considerable DNA and hormonal data that cause people to be born gay.

My novel also contains a second part - **Part 2**: a science fiction novel that describes both imaginary and workable technics intended to achieve a conversion from homosexuality to heterosexuality and from lesbianism to "straight" women. These proposed scientific technics are based on my personal scientific training and on sound contemporary scientific procedures.

For the writing the essay, I used information taken from various articles on the Internet. For this information, I want to thank the contributors. I had to use the Internet because I am a layperson, a dilettante – I am neither a psychologist nor an M.D. - I "just" have a Ph.D. degree in Microbiology. In addition, I must say that I am a retired person, and have a "strange" penchant for writing and trying to publish science fiction novels…

NOTE: the genuine scientific data that I brought below, is intertwined with the science fiction part that came from my "feverish mind." As a result, facts (from my scientific training) and science Fiction are mixed inseparably together...

Chapter 1:
The Scientist

Professor Jack Hunter, a tall balding man in his sixties, with finely chiseled face, a mustache, and a beard, sat in his office which was in the Psychology department of the University of California (Berkeley).

The wall behind his back held several rows of certificates and honorary memberships of scientific societies, as well as calfskin parchments of important prizes that he garnered during his past research work. On his desk was a photograph of his family showing his wife and two sons. One slightly larger silver-framed photograph showed a pretty baby, a granddaughter.

Professor Hunter was not remarkably busy ever since he stepped down from the chair of the Psychology Department. This stepping-down occurred because he became tired of bureaucratic matters: the need to beg for budgets and donations for the department, the political squabbles of his colleagues and their scrambling for positions. In addition to his stepping down, he also reduced his research activities, and because of his partial retirement from research, he did not apply any more for research grants.

True, he kept a small laboratory with one post-doctoral fellow, one computer-coding specialist, and one expert statistician, and he still performed some research work. However, he was quite content with his past scientific achievements and felt that he deserved to sit on his laurels and follow the work of the new scientists who were inspired by his past ground-breaking discoveries. In about one hour he was going to teach a class for graduate students entitled "The scientific basis of Gender preferences" (Psychology 205). Therefore, he used the spare time till the lecture to proof-read a short article that he wrote at the request of the editor of the science section of the 'Berkley Gazette." The editor was Tim Fruman, who studied for a master's degree under his coaching and stayed his friend. Following is a transcript of Professor Hunter's article from the "gazette":

The factors that induce homosexuality, lesbianism, and transgenderism
By Professor jack Hunter,
The department of Psychology, university of California (Berkley)

"Many discoveries were made in the in the last 30 years that helped scientists to elucidate the factors that induce the appearance of the members of the third gender – gays, lesbians, and transgenders. Let me summarize them briefly for you. They prove that the presence of members of the third gender is caused by the effect of genes and hormones and is not the result of willing, learned, depravity.

I. Factors inducing homosexuality:

Ia. Genetic factors:
The first discovery of the effect of genetic factors (genes) on the sexual orientation of gay people was made in 1986, by a scientist named Professor Dean Hamer, from the National Cancer Institute in Bethesda, Maryland. Hamer and his collaborators studied 51 brothers of gay men coming from the maternal side of the family and 50 brothers of gay men from the paternal side of the family. The number of gay brothers of gay men from the paternal side was like the number of gay people in the general population. However, the number of the gay brothers of gay men <u>from the maternal side</u> was four times

higher than their rate in the general population. This showed that there is a homosexuality-inducing gene (or genes) <u>on the X chromosome</u> since during fertilization, which produces an XY baby, the X chromosome is transferred only from the mother. An added study showed that this/these gene(s) are in the <u>Xq28 region of the X chromosome.</u> Another site for a homosexuality gene was later identified in the peri-centromeric region (around the chromosomal centromere[1]) of chromosome 8 of the mother's chromosome complement.

Ib. Hormonal factor(s):
The proof that I shall cite here, comes from the observation of the "Fraternal birth order effect." In this effect, it was found that the more grown-up brothers a baby has, the greater is the chance that he may be born gay person. Every existing grown-up brother in the family increases by 33% the chance that the next newborn baby will be gay. The best hypothesis to explain this phenomenon is that the immune system of the mother becomes increasingly active with each next exposure to the fetuses in her womb. As a result, her immune system produces antibodies against some yet unknown, important heterosexuality-inducing male hormones.

Ic. Parental effect:
Many gay people mention the absence of a father-figure in their lives. Their fathers always worked late or left the family entirely or treated their sons cruelly and with extreme harsh discipline.

II. Factors inducing lesbianism:

IIa. genetic factor:
A study showing that there is a gene or genes that induce lesbianism was conducted by Michael Bayley and Richard Pillard of the Boston University, School of Medicine. These scientists studied lesbian female twins resulting from a single split fertilized ovum (monozygotic twins) and compared them to pairs of twins born from two different ova (dizygotic twins). They found that all pairs of twins coming from a single split ovum were lesbian. However, in many cases, only one girl in the twins coming from two different ova was

lesbian and the second one was not. This proves that lesbianism was induced genetically.

IIb. Hormonal factor(s):
Hormones also play a key role in causing the type of sexual orientation of gays, lesbians, and transgenders. The hormonal theory of sexuality dictates that, just as exposure to certain hormones decides the gender of the fetus, exposure to other hormones influences the sexual orientation of the adult. For instance, many lesbians carry a male hormone called Testosterone in their bloodstream, while non-lesbians do not. Androgen (another male hormone) also plays a part in inducing their lesbian sexual orientation. Many lesbians underwent sexual assaults by members of their closest family - a factor that caused them to turn to lesbianism.

III. Factors inducing Transgenderism

Transgenderism is an unfortunate mistake of Nature: births of persons with the bodies of one gender, with an overwhelming need to convert into the opposite gender. This conversion is achieved with the help of hormones and surgery.

When professor Hunter finished his proof-reading, he sent the article by e-mail to Fruman and received back a "thank-you" mail. Fruman also wrote that he is going to send Hunter, by regular mail, an honorarium paycheck for the article in the sum of 100 dollars. Professor Hunter refused the check since it would force him to go to the bank to cash it. In the back-mail professor Hunter suggested a trout fishing date on the coming Sunday which Furman accepted.

This matter over, Professor Hunter had ten minutes left to read his notes in preparation for the first lecture. When he was satisfied that his coming lecture was well entrenched in his memory, and that the time for his lecture drew extremely near, he went to the auditorium which was already full. Professor Hunter was used to many listeners, even among those who were not studying for a graduate degree.

On the podium already stood Professor Dan Henriké, the current Chairman of the psychology department. Professor Henriké waited until the last late student sat down and then said:

"Dear Students,

I am not in the habit of introducing a lecturer from our department before the teaching of his classes. However, this is an exception. The Psychology Department is proud to number Professor Hunter among its ranks. He is well known for his pioneering work on the etiology of homosexuality and lesbianism. His studies had led to the conclusion that these sexual orientations are, at least in part, genetically inherited, and that they are not a learned, willing choice.

In the early 1990's, Hunter and Pillard co-authored a series of studies on male twins that examined the rate of gay identity among monozygotic male twins born from a splitting of a single fertilized ovum. These monozygotic twins had a homosexuality incidence rate of 52%. Dizygotic male twins (born from two different fertilized ova) had a homosexuality incidence rate of 22%. Non-twin siblings and adopted siblings showed 11% homosexuality incidence rate. The Non-twin male siblings and adopted non-twin male siblings served as negative controls. These findings showed that homosexuality may be transferred through a gene or genes from the mother.

In addition, Professor Hunter also studied lesbianism. By using ads in the gay mass media, he found, together with Pillard, 147 lesbians of which 115 had twin sisters and 32 that had non-twin sisters. Both sister groups were born to lesbian mothers and each pair had been raised together in the same homes. Among the identical monozygotic twin girls, who shared an identical genetic inheritance, forty-eight percent of them were lesbians. Among the non-twin, dizygotic sisters, who did not share an identical genetic inheritance with the other sisters, only sixteen percent of the pairs of these sisters were lesbians. This showed that there is a genetic basis also to lesbianism. Professor Hunter contributed many more important studies which I shall not cite, since I do not want to take over the whole lesson. I shall just add that he had served as chairperson of the Department until October 2016. Currently, Professor Hunter is mostly engaged in teaching. Now without a further ado, I give you Professor Hunter."

Professor Hunter climbed to the podium, picked up the microphone that was relinquished by Professor Henriké, and started to speak:

"Dear students,

Many lecturers and speakers feel obliged to start their lectures or talks with a funny witticism or a joke to "break the ice." I had already given the present course three years running and still need find a good starting "ice breaker." I challenge all of you now to produce throughout the coming semester such a brilliant starting joke or witticism that relates to sex and its deviant forms. The prize for such a find would be the addition of twenty grade points to the result of the final exam of the successful author or authoress. Every student can send only one joke or witticism to my E-mailbox that you can find in the faculty's roster. Sending of more than one attempt will result in a complete deletion of all the suggestions of the male or female transgressing student, plus an immediate reduction of ten points from the result if his/her final exam. I shall use the winning joke in my next course, God willing.

However, right now, listen to my lecture and do not burden your brains with attempts to produce joke or a witticism, just now. You will have a whole semester for that. I know that it will be difficult for you to stop just now thinking about a joke. That is because if you tell a person not to think throughout a session about, say, a pink elephant carrying a colored balloon tied to his trunk, he will not stop thinking about it…

Chapter 2:
The Professor Teaches...

After throwing the gauntlet of the joke, Professor Hunter started his lecture:

"In the first and second lectures of the course I shall discuss the subject of homosexuality. The three lectures following these two lectures will be devoted to lesbianism. What will happen after that I still have not yet decided."

Suddenly there was a knock on the door and a secretary entered. She whispered something in the professor ear. The professor made one step back in tension, thought for a minute and then he said:

"Dan, can you do me a big favor and take over the lecture for me? Something important came up and I must leave. Luckily, it is not any tragic event." The dean looked up in surprise but nodded, , stood up and went to replace Professor Hunter on the podium. Professor Hunter never received a successful witticism from his students, since at next lecture, the students entered the lecture hall, and found the following notice on their lecterns:

"Dear students,

At the start of the first lecture, I have received before your very eyes, a notice on the acceptance of an exceptionally large research grant that causes me to undertake an excessively intensive research project. This means that I will have to stop teaching your course at its very beginning. Luckily, Professor Emeritus Edward Kent agreed to come out of his retirement and teach the course instead of me. Professor Kent is an excellent teacher and scientist. In fact, he taught the course before me, and I replaced him when he retired.

I wish you an immense success in the present course, and with Professor Kent's teaching , you are bound to succeed.

Signed: Professor Jack Hunter

Chapter 3:
The evangelist sponsor

The circumstances that caused Professor Hunter to stop teaching were quite extraordinary, and were as follows: At the secretary's behest, he went to his office and found there a letter marked three times, on various places on the envelope, with the notice "urgent," "urgent," urgent." The signer on the letter was completely unknown to him, with the name of John Donner. The subject appeared at the top of the letter which read: **"A very large grant privately endowed"**

This is what the letter said:

"Honorable Professor Hunter,

My name is Armand Donner. I am and an evangelist. My son is an evangelist too and <u>a gay person</u>. He knows that his condition is not due to his fault but was genetically decreed. However, I am a preacher and the head of my church, and he knows that his sexual orientation, if known, will hurt my position in my parish. Therefore, he asked me to approach some genetic scientists in his name and ask them, if it is possible, to "convert him" to heterosexuality.

I had been blessed from God with a large fortune derived from oil fields and oil wells in Oklahoma. These wells were claimed by my family many years ago when they first came as pioneers to Oklahoma. You can find my name in a list of the richest tycoons in the USA.

As I said above, I want to help my son and to "convert" him heterosexuality, if it is at all possible.

Aside from my son's wish to help me in my vocation, I would also love to get grandchildren fathered by him; he is my only son... Therefore, I plan to endow a scientist with a large grant if he will agree to try to find a way to convert my son to heterosexuality. I checked around and all the geneticists and psychologists that I approached pointed to you and praised your ability and your scientific interest in Homosexuality. Hence my present mail.

Please, will you agree to make the effort to try to convert my son and his male progeny? If you agree to make the effort, please answer by email, or call me on my personal number (405-366-8012).

Best regards, Armand Donner

Donner's request touched on an important subject that had been nagging many geneticists and psychologists. Professor Hunter himself was sure that he could solve the matter of conversion. However, before the tycoon's mail, he had felt that he was "burned out" and disliked starting again the race to obtain grants for the study of the problem. Besides, he was getting near to retirement. Therefore, he had decided in the past, to transfer the solution of the conversion problem to younger researchers.

However, when Donner's offer of a huge grant appeared to fall into his lap like a ripe fruit, all his old instincts woke up and he felt the urge to return to research. He at once felt like he received a new lease on life!

As a first step, Professor Hunter wanted to find information on Donner's self-proclaimed fortune and his character. He opened Wikipedia and this is what he read:

"Early oil history in Oklahoma: Oil seeps were recognized in Oklahoma long before the arrival of the European settlers, who mined some seeps for asphalt. The first subsurface oil was recovered in 1859 by accident, near present-day Salinas, in a well drilled for water. Its small amount of oil was sold for use in lamps. More oil came from a well drilled in 1889 in an area of seeps near Chelsea (Rogers County). The well generated half a barrel of oil per day and was used as "dip oil" to treat cattle for ticks (Franks, 1980). The first commercial paying well, the "Nellie No. 1", was drilled in 1896 near Bartlesville (Washington County). The giant Bartlesville oil field, in which "Nellie No. 1" is found, lied in a land staked by Otto Donner in 1890. Now the Donners own the sole rights to the huge Bartlesville Field.

The "Nellie No. 1" oil well ushered in the oil era for Oklahoma Territory and added Billions of dollars to the bank accounts of the Donner family. Production in the Bartlesville Field, and in other areas, rose rapidly thereafter and added much impetus towards the granting of Statehood to Oklahoma in 1907. In the years between the first discovery of the well and Statehood, Oklahoma became the biggest oil-producing state in the USA.

Nowadays, the ownership of the Bartlesville oil fields belongs to Donner's great grandson, Armand Donner, who is the head of the donner family and owns about 70% of the heritage of Otto Donner. Several more distant relatives of the family also own some oil fields.

Armand Donner is a fervent evangelist and had donated a huge fortune to further the cause of evangelism in the USA and abroad. He also built a large evangelistic church with his own rich resources and serves as the pastor in that church.

The professor browsed among Donner's sermons and his eyes struck a sample of one of Donner's sermons that dealt with the subject of homosexuality:" Hunter read the sermon, to get a better understanding of Donner's views on the matter:

"Dear fellow worshipers,

I would like to devote my present sermon to homosexuality, otherwise also known as "gayness". Here are some quotes from the scriptures and the Quran that call homosexuality a sin before God. A sin which needs to be punished:

Some quotes from the Old Testament:

Genesis 19:4-13: "Before they had gone to bed, all the men from every part of the city of Sodom - both young and old - surrounded the house. They called to Lot, "Where are the men who came to you tonight? Bring them out to us so that we can have sex with them".

Leviticus 18:22: "Thou shalt not lie with mankind, as with womankind: it is an abomination."

Leviticus 20:13: "If a man lies with a male as with a woman, both of them have committed an abomination; they shall surely be put to death; their blood is upon them."

Deuteronomy 22:5: "A woman must not put on men's clothing, and a man must not wear women's clothing. Anyone who does this is detestable in the sight of the Lord your God."

Some quotes from the New Testament

1Corinthians 6:9-11: "Do not be deceived: neither the sexually immoral, nor idolaters, nor adulterers, nor men who practice gayety, nor thieves, nor the greedy, nor drunkards, nor revilers, nor swindlers will inherit the kingdom of God".

Jude 1:7: "Just as Sodom and Gomorrah and the surrounding cities, which likewise indulged in sexual immorality and pursued unnatural desire, will serve as an example by undergoing a punishment of eternal fire".

1Timothy 1:8-10: "The law is not laid down for the just, but for the lawless and disobedient, for the ungodly and sinners, for the unholy and profane, for those who strike their fathers and mothers, for murderers, the sexually immoral, men who practice gayety, the enslavers, liars, perjurers, and whatever else is contrary to sound doctrine."

Some quotes from Islamic sources And the Quran:

The Quran calls homosexuality "coming with lust" to men instead of women (or their wives) and calls it an abomination. (Quran 7:80-84) "For ye practice your lusts on men in preference to women: ye are indeed a people transgressing beyond bounds. And we shall rain down on them a shower of brimstone".

The biblical story of Sodom is also repeated in three other Suras (chapters) of the Quran: 15:74, 27:58 and 29:40.

Quran (26:165-166): "Of all the creatures in the world, will ye approach males, and leave those whom Allah has created for you to be your mates? Nay, ye are a people transgressing".

Mohammed's first successor, Abu Bakr, had a gay person burned at the stake. The fourth caliph, Mohammed's son-in-law Ali, ordered a 'sodomite' thrown down from the minaret of a mosque and other homosexuals he ordered to be stoned.

One of the earliest and most authoritative commentators on the Quran, Ibn Abbas, blended both approaches into a two-step execution in which "the 'sodomite' should be thrown from the highest building in the town and then stoned".

"Currently, in many Islamic nations, where Islam's laws are most strictly applied, gay people are still oppressed and are many times, in danger for their lives.

Despite the ancient quotations from the scriptures and the Quran that I brought just now, I had many discussions with my Bishop and several elders and all of them feel that our dear evangelism needs to undergo a change in doctrine with regards to gayness. We cannot continue to hold ideas that disregard science completely!!

Science has found that that homosexuality is not a sin and is not a learned perversion or a willing decision, but one that appears because the existence of two human genes that were discovered by the scientists. Same-sex attraction is also induced in in the womb by hormones. When this discovery became known, many gay people became reconciled with their heredity and do not want to change it. If such a possibility existed. Also, public opinion towards homosexuality has mostly swerved, and gay people are now accepted with equanimity in quite a few countries of the world. Only ignorant, unenlightened people keep deep animosity towards gay people and persecute them, unhindered by the police. Gay men still suffer from unemployment and cannot serve in the armies of some countries.

Some of you know that my only son, Jack, is a sophomore in Oklahoma University. He is an 'A' student, a substitute quarterback, and a strong athlete; However, I want to divulge to you that he is also gay, **and I am not ashamed on this score**."

Here Donner stopped his sermon to let his statement sink in, and to allow some time for the cries of surprise and shock to subside. When silence came back, he continued: "since he is a devout evangelist like me, he wants to get rid of his sexual tendency - he wants to become 'sexually pure' and to obey the ancient dictates of the scriptures. Despite my views that do not consider homosexuality to be a sin, I have decided to help him to convert to heterosexuality. I shall undertake the task of contacting the best scientists in the field to do the job! This is because all the psychiatric and psychological treatments in the world cannot achieve true conversion."

Here Donner left the subject of homosexuality and continued with the usual evangelistic exhortation: "Know ye that the word 'gospel' means good news.

Many well-meaning Christians begin their evangelistic efforts with the 'good news' of God's love for humankind. However, this message is lost on the unbelievers who must first comet to grips with the extent of the 'sad news,' before they return to God:

First, man is separated from a holy, righteous God by sin. Second, God hates sin and is angry with the wicked every day. Third, death and judgment are inevitable, as said in Hebrews 9:27. Fourth, man is incapable of doing anything about the situation. Until the full extent of this 'sad news' happens to him, the 'good news', cannot be communicated.

Only when we understand how holy and just God is, we can begin to understand His hatred of sin and His righteous wrath against sinners and those who are bigoted. The sins that God hates are pride, lying, murder, false witness, those who stir up trouble, and those with evil in their hearts."

Here Professor Hunter stopped reading the sermon. He felt that it gave him an understanding of Donner's character and his aim. The Professor reflected for a few minutes, but he did not have to consider the offer too long. When Donner's offer of a huge grant came, he felt the old urge to return to do research again!

Chapter 4:
The Scientist meet the evangelist

The professor wrote back a mail to Donner, saying that he wants to work on the problem. He also said that he already has some ideas how to tackle it. He added his phone number and waited eagerly for a reply.

Donner, overjoyed, answered Hunter within the hour by phone, and invited him to his offices. He asked Professor Hunter whether he would agree to fly to meet him. In this case, he said, he will send a limousine to take him to Oakland's International Airport and from there his private jet will fly him to Will Rogers World Airport in Oklahoma City. Finally, he said, another limousine will take him to his offices. When Professor Hunter agreed, all that remained was to fix a date. It so happened, that Professor Hunter was free from classes the next day, and since both men were very eager to meet, their meeting was quickly set for the next day, 12 noon, Oklahoma time.

However, Professor Hunter did not sleep too well in the night before the meeting. He kept turning in his mind his acceptance of Donner's offer. Lying besides his wife, the night's inactivity and lack of sleep have dyed Donner's offer in a more realistic shade. Doubts swarmed in his mind as to whether he should accept the offer and start an ambitious new project at his ripe age of 65 years. In two years, he will be entitled to retirement. He liked Golf and fishing which he felt were more proper for a "mature man,' rather than long hours again in the lab and conference room. Was he up to it? Finally, he decided to call Donner in the morning and withdraw from his earlier agreement. Only after this decision, he finally fell asleep.

In the morning, he woke his wife, explained the situation, and asked her opinion on the matter. Being certain that Flora, his wife, would agree to his rejection of Donner's offer. He was completely surprised at her reaction: Flora encouraged him to take the project, even though she knew that it meant long hours in the lab in which she would barely see him! "Jack, my dear!" She said: "You cannot fight your nature and character! You are a committed research scientist, and nothing will change that. You must agree to take the job! If you will not accept it, after a few months in retirement, you will get bored of inactivity. As for me, I knew what life we are going to lead when I married you! You have my heartfelt approval. I am sure that if you reject the job, you will rue it up to your last breath."

Hunter looked at Flora, mumbled a few half-hearted objections, and finally accepted the inevitable...

He packed up a light suitcase with a pair of pajamas and a travel kit for his toiletry things since he did not know how long his business with Donner would take. After a few minutes of waiting, a chauffeur rang at the door of his apartment. He kissed Flora, and off he went...

The chauffeur drove to Oakland's international airport and straight to the area where Donner's Gulfstream G-650 jet plane was already waiting for him. The two pilots of the plane rose early in the morning and managed to cross the 1250 miles from Will Rogers

World Airport to Oakland's International Airport in about two and a half hours.

The professor had flown to scientific conferences, to invited lectures, or to vacations with his family, only in 'business class.' On his salary, he could not afford to fly 'First Class", except when once an over-booking forced a stewardess to lead him to a 'First Class' seat in one of his flights. When he was supposed to present a paper in a conference, or serve as a chairperson of a session, his fare and lodging was paid from a grant that he had received, or by the conference organizers, but with a thrifty limit. Therefore, he examined his surrounding and thought to himself that Donner travelled in a new flight class – 'billionaire class'…

Donner's private jet was very spacious and was flown by two pilots, but the second pilot was necessary only in case that the first pilot became somehow incapacitated. Therefore, the second pilot was free to act as an air steward and welcomed Professor Hunter. First, he offered him Champagne that Hunter declined. Then he offered him a breakfast or lunch from the galley. Again, Hunter declined since he wanted to sit quietly in the comfortable armchair that he chose in the Jet's salon. He wanted to collect his thoughts and to prepare for the meeting with Donner.

When the flight was over, a pilot helped him down the steps and he entered an elegant limousine that brought him to Donner's offices in 610 Parrington Oval Str., Norman, Oklahoma.

Donner, who followed Hunter's progress along the route by phone to the various transporters, waited eagerly at the door of his office to welcome him. He at once shook Hunter's hand warmly with both hands.

He was a slight, respectable looking man in his fifties, with silver hair and keen eyes. Along the way to Donner's office, Hunter passed no less than three secretaries, and each one was prettier than the former one. Donner apologized for this show-off and said that this is expected of him in his business…

Donner said: "Professor Hunter, it is an intense pleasure to meet you. Did you have a good flight?"

Hunter, after a quick inspection of Donner said: "I, too, am pleased to meet you, Mr. Donner, and I look forward to a fruitful discussion. Yes, my flight to your place was as smooth as a Single Malt Scotch Whiskey, as the saying goes..."

Donner said: "Speaking of whiskey, what would you like to drink? I have a well-stocked bar. In addition, can I order lunch for both of us from an excellent caterer whose services I often use?"

Hunter skipped breakfast in the morning and declined the pilot's proposal of a meal in flight. Therefore, he was glad to accept Donner's offer of lunch. He was led to the company's conference room, and he let Donner order. Soon, the large oval conference table was filled by two waiters with all sorts of foods and drinks. While eating, Donner said: "Professor Hunter, may I call you Jack?

Hunter answered: "why, certainly, but on condition that I call you Armand?" Donner said: "Of course, I insist, but no, not Armand. Call me Yohan, please. My family and all my friends call me by this name. The roots of my family are Germanic – they emigrated from Westphalia to Oklahoma in the nineteenth century. I would gladly like to number you among my friends, so Yohan it will be…"

Chapter 5:
The Evangelist billionaire expresses a wish and the professor complies

The two men finished lunch and the waiters came and cleared the Conference table. Then Donner looked eagerly, and with an undisguised concern at Hunter and said: "Now Jack, with your permission, I know that I am asking you to perform nothing less than a miracle. Still, I would like to hear from you, in lay terms, how do you plan to work on our problem. Can it be solved at all? What are the chances for obtaining a conversion?"

Hunter looked at Donner, saw how much his son's sexual orientation meant to him, and he carefully weighed his words. Scientifically, the problem of "conversion" of a gay person challenged him and appealed to him. He also felt that it would add to his reputation if he solved it. However, for the life of him, he could not understand Donner's compulsion. Being a gay person did not seem to him so much of a problem. Gay people are now accepted as natural equals in the USA without prejudice, even by many members of the clergy. However, on further thought he understood the cultural milieu of evangelism in which Yohan existed. He decided to work hard on the problem, and Donner's money will help him to get much help in his work. Once he reached this realization, in him, he said:

"Well Yohan, let me put it this way: The chances of success outweigh those of failure! This is because in the last 20 years, science had progressed in a geometric pace. Tens of thousands of scientists, in all fields, have added a lot understanding and marvelous technologies to all sciences. As a result, I think that only the sky is the limit. However, that is only if the Carbon Dioxide in our skies will not lead us to our doom in the next fifty years!... I promise you that I will do my best to solve our problem with the help of some of the most advanced technologies and with the best up-and-coming young scientists. They will help me with disciplines in which I am less proficient. Let me now describe to you what would be my first line of attack."

Hunter collected his thoughts and then decided that the best way to explain to Donner his future attempts to convert gays to heterosexuality will be to fall back to some materials from his lectures of the Psychology 205 course. And to add some innovations that he thought of recently. At first, he decided to give Yohan some idea about the state of the DNA that turns people to same sex preference. He cleared his throat and started his discourse:

"Yohan, before I enter the exposition of the future ways that I and my hired scientists may undertake, I am going to summarize to you the current state of the art:

There is no single gene that determines a person's sexual orientation. However, a massive new study shows that genetics — along with the environment, hormones — play a part in shaping sexuality. Researchers analyzed DNA from hundreds of thousands of people and found that there are a handful of genes clearly connected with same-sex sexual behavior. The researchers say that, although variations in these genes cannot predict whether a person is gay, these variants may partly influence sexual behavior.

Andrea Ganna, lead author and European Molecular Biology Laboratory group leader at the Institute of Molecular Medicine in Finland, said that the research that I shall soon describe to you reinforces the understanding that homosexuality is simply "a natural part of our diversity as a species."

His new study and that of his colleagues is not the first to explore the link between genetics and homosexuality, but it is the largest of its kind, and experts say that it provides one of the clearest pictures of genes and sexuality.

With an international team of scientists, Ganna, who is also an instructor at Massachusetts General and Harvard, examined data from more than 470,000 people in the United States and the United Kingdom to see whether certain genetic markers in their DNA were linked to their sexual behavior. Specifically, the researchers used data from the UK Biobank study and from the private genomics company "23 and Me", which contained their DNA data and responses to questions about sexual behaviors, sexual attraction, and sexual orientation.

Professor hunter continued: "More than 26,000 participants reported at least one sexual encounter with someone of the same sex. Earlier studies, the researchers said, were not large enough to reveal the subtle effects of individual genes.

The researchers were able to find five genetic variants that were statistically associated with homosexual behaviors.

However, none had a large effect, and none could, by itself predict homosexual behaviors. One of the variants was found in a stretch of DNA that includes several genes related to the sense of smell. Another one of the genes is related to male pattern baldness, which the authors said could suggest that sex hormone regulation may somehow be involved.

The analysis showed that these variants, along with thousands of others in the human genome that have even smaller effects, together accounted for 8 to 25 percent of variation in homosexual behavior.

Some of the variants were correlated with homosexual behavior in men, others in women, and some in both. The above study marks the end of "the simplistic concept of one 'gay gene.'"

"It just shows us that homosexual behavior is much more complex than this idea of having just one gene influencing it all," said the professor. "It shows that there are genetic factors, which we had suspected long ago … but it also shows those genetic factors do not tell the whole story."

"Previous studies have suggested that sexual orientation and homosexual behaviors may be, at least in part, genetic. For instance, research has shown patterns in families with multiple men in the same family identifying as gay. There is some evidence of a correlation between left-handedness and blue eye color and same-sex attraction. Also, environmental effects may be a factor for some people.

Zeke Stokes, a scientist who had been active in the study of gay chromosome variants, said that the new research on the genetics of variants "provides even more evidence that being gay, or lesbian is a natural part of human life, a conclusion that has been drawn by researchers and scientists repeatedly. The identities of LGBTQ people are not up for debate. This new research also reconfirms the long-established understanding that there is no conclusive degree to which nature - or nurture- influence how a gay or lesbian person behaves."

The Professor continued:

"Now I am going to describe to you some of the methods used by the various scientists to study some of the causative genetic factors of same-sex attraction. It is true that they do not give any hint how to work on the conversion problem of your son, but they give an idea how difficult it is to study gay people.

In the description of each method, I shall bring the results obtained, the name of the responsible scientist who achieved the results, and in some cases, the year in which the results were obtained.

Chapter 6:
Population studies intended to show that DNA is the culprit

<u>Method No. 1</u>: Population genetics: – comparing groups of gay people coming from the maternal side of the family to those coming from the paternal side. There are two variations of the method that were used by the scientists and their colleagues.

<u>Method 1A:</u> - Determination of the incidence of homosexuality among <u>brothers</u> of gay men from the <u>maternal side</u> to the incidence of homosexuality in <u>brothers</u> of gay men from the <u>paternal side</u>. An increased incidence of homosexuality in brothers from the maternal side, compared to that of brothers from the paternal side, will show that there might be a gene or genes on chromosome X that handles the occurrence of homosexuality in those maternal-side brothers. This is because males always inherit their chromatid of the X chromosome from their mothers.

This study, which was carried out by Dean H. Hamer and colleagues from the National Institutes of health in 1986, showed that the number of gay brothers of gay people from the maternal side, was four times higher than the incidence of gay people in the general population. The number of gay brothers of gay people from the paternal side, was low and was like the rate of gay people in the general population.

Method 1B: - Determination of the incidence of homosexuality among cousins of gay uncles from the maternal side, compared to cousins of gay uncles from the paternal side. This study, which was again carried out by Dean H. Hamer, showed an increased incidence of homosexuality in cousins of uncles from the maternal side, but not from the paternal side. This, as with method 1A, suggested that there might be a gene, or genes, on chromosome X that are responsible for the induction of homosexuality. Again: because males always inherit their copy of the X chromosome, with its homosexuality gene(s), from their mothers.

Method 2: This is a straightforward method – Determination of the sizes of whole brains and the weights of their amygdalae in straight and gay cadavers. in 1991, the geneticist Simon LeVay found differences in the brain sizes and the weights of amygdalae between gay and straight men. The sizes and weights of these organs in gay people were smaller than the same organs in straight people. The amygdala is an almond-shaped mass of gray matter inside both cerebral hemispheres which is involved with the experiencing of emotion.

Method 3: Determination of polymorphisms in the X chromosome. Polymorphism is the existence of a gene having two or more different appearances that were caused by mutations in a single nucleotide, or in a polynucleotide, or in a whole gene. For example, there are 2 polymorphisms in a jaguar's skin coloring: it can have light-polymorphic coloring or dark-polymorphic coloring. One of the ways to study Polymorphisms is by a method called "chromosome linkage." Sit conveniently in your armchair because I am now going to present to you a long description of the method:

One mode of "chromosome linkage" is called crossing-over. This mode will yield a composite female x chromatid (single DNA strand) This composite single female X chromatid has in some location along its length, a DNA piece from the X chromatid of the male in a connection (linkage). This process happens during the production of sex gametes called meiosis. Professor Hunter now opened his laptop, rummaged a little and showed donner the following drawing:

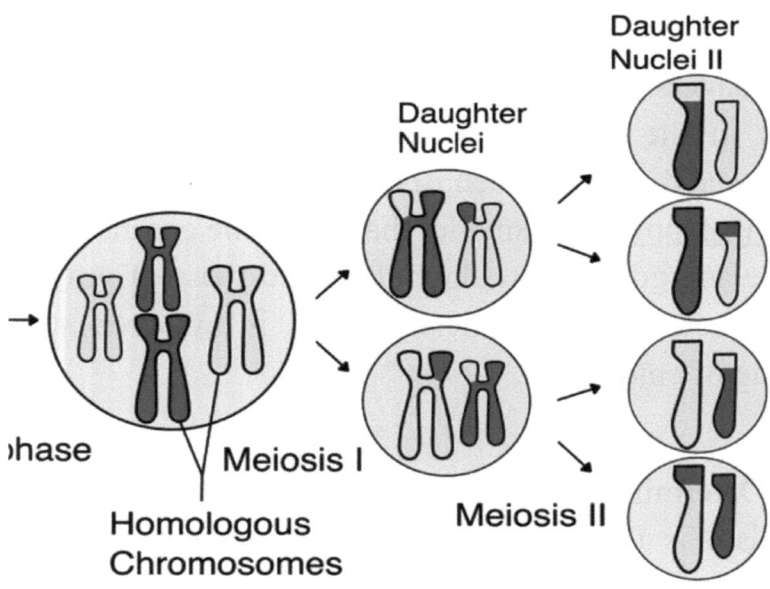

Crossed- over double and single stranded

DNA Chromosomes and Chromatids

containing A Male DNA pieces

Then he said: "the process in the figure is called **meiosis**. This process yields at its end gametes (single stranded sperm cells or ova) that take part in our human multiplication.

I want to apologize to you on the fact that meiosis is a bit complicated process that requires a long description. So here goes: before fertilization, in a stage called meiosis # 1, there occurs a doubling of the number of double-stranded DNA chromosomes in the cell that is destined to become at the end of the two meiosises (#1 and #2) a single stranded sperm cell or a single stranded DNA (chromatid)-containing ovum.

The **meiosis # 1** yields on one hand two male gametes (sex cells) that have two complements of double-stranded male chromosomes with two Y chromosomes, (blue in the scheme below). On the other hand, it also yields two Female gametes with two complements of female chromosomes which have two X chromosomes (red in the scheme).

Then comes meiosis # 2 in which the resulting two types of "fat" gametes (male and female from meiosis 1) split in two to give two male and two female daughter gametes, but each male gamete now has a single male chromatid (Y) and single female chromatid (X) in the scheme). In this stage there occurs a splitting of the double stranded chromosomes in each of the 2 gametes <u>along their lengths</u>, plus a multiplication to produce 4 single stranded sex gametes (chromatids). Each of these gametes has one complete Y chromatid (red chromatid) and one complete X chromatid (blue chromatid). The four gametes are sex cells – sperm cells if they are produced in the testes, or ova if they are produced in the ovaries.

Now I need to speak about the crossing-over. In meiosis # 1, there often occurs a process of the "crossing over." In it, the X chromatid of the male that has a gay polymorphism from a gay father, exchanges piece with a piece of the X chromatid of the female that has a "normal" (wild type) polymorphism. This happens in a region of the female chromatid called Xq28. The result is a composite female gamete (ovum) with an X chromatid that has two parts in it (one long part from the original long X chromatid and one short male Y gay piece from the crossing-over). This 'composite' female with a GAY Y piece will eventually mate with a Y sperm to yield a gay baby boy (its DNA will contain a normal Y chromatid and a crossed-over female X chromatid with a gay male Y piece).

The normal part of female chromatid which has a Xq28 region may either overlap with the male crossed-over Xq28 piece with its homosexuality inducing part during the crossing over, or they may reside slightly apart from each other, or much further from each other.

The distance between the normal part of Xq28 in the X chromatid of the female, and the homosexuality Xq28 part of gene derived by crossing over from the Y gene is determined by a computerized "chromosome linkage" method called the "LOD score chromosome linkage". Dean H. Hamer tested forty pairs of gay twins for the presence of the male-derived crossed-over X piece (which is in the Xq28 region). and found that thirty-three gay twins had the gay polymorphisms. The polymorphisms of the twins showed a significantly greater existence of gay persons (33/40 =82.5%) than that which can just be explained by Mendelian segregation in the general population. Therefore this, again, showed that a genetic link to homosexuality does exist.

The Xq28 region is a large, complex, and gene-dense region. Among its various genes are twelve genes of the melanoma-associated antigens (MAGE) family. In this family there is the MAGEA11 gene that had been identified as a co-regulator for the androgen receptor.

Dr. Hu, conducted. in Hamer's lab in 1995, an added "LOD chromosome linkage" study with a bigger sample of gay twins. This study corroborated the results of Professor Hamer that gay twins share a significantly elevated rates of crossed-over polymorphic Y piece in the long female X chromosome. Straight brothers who were also tested, showed a significantly smaller sharing of the crossed-over polymorphic homosexuality sequence. No linkage at all- was found in the Xq28 region of lesbian females indicating that lesbians have a different genetic pathway for their sexual preference. A later analysis by Hu replicated and refined his earlier findings. This study revealed that 67% of gay twins shared polymorphic crossed-over homosexuality sequences in the Xq28 region.

Moreover, several independent investigators supported in 2012 the existence of a polymorphic homosexuality gene in the Xq28 region. However, in addition, they also found a second polymorphic gene of Gay sexual behavior in the peri-centromeric (round the chromosomal centromere) region of chromosome 8. As I already described to you previously. Their study population comprised of 409 pairs of gay brothers, who were analyzed in in the LOD chromosome linkage test with over 300,000 single-nucleotide linkage markers.

Method 4: The PCR method: This is a very advanced form of the "chromosome linkage" method which was performed by Dr. Rice. This method is so important for many types of analyses, such as crime fighting, detection of viruses, the determination of the markers of diseases, and much more. As a result, the inventors of the PCR method were awarded a Nobel Prize! To perform the PCR (Polymerase Chain Reaction method), the double stranded DNAs from the cells of the tested persons, or saliva, or a DNA stain left in a crime scene, etc., are extracted, and "denatured"[1]. Then, specific 'DNA primers' are added to the reaction mixture. These "DNA primers" are short single-stranded DNA pieces, which had been chemically synthesized and are specific "starters" and "enders" of the gene(s) targeted for study. They supply boundaries for replication so that only the part of the chromatid sequestered between the 2 primers is copied. Together with the primers that attached themselves to the "sense" chromatid and sequester (define) it, a <u>heat-resistant DNA polymerase enzyme</u> is added. It replicates the sequestered-targeted chromatid DNA gene that needs to be studied into a double stranded DNA. To achieve this replication, four Deoxynucleotides triphosphates that are tagged with fluorescein dye are added. Repetitive PCR reaction cycles are started and promote the synthesis of <u>millions of copies</u> of complementary double stranded, fluorescein-stained, DNA pieces of the gene(s) studied. The repetitive PCR reactions are performed in an automated cycling machine. It exposes the reactants to repeated cycles of heating and cooling to create successive temperature-dependent reactions: (step 1) DNA denaturation: separation into single stranded chromatids, and (step 2) polymerase-driven DNA replications, and back again to the DNA denaturation and so on. The fluorescent-labeled amplified targeted genes are next separated after their replications according to their size and electric charge on an agar block (gel), while driven by an

---

[1] Separated by heat to obtain their single strands [chromatids].

electric field. This separation process is called 'Electrophoresis.' The separated fluorescent-labeled targeted genes are readily visualized under UV light on the agar block after the electrophoresis. The lengths of the isolated specific DNA pieces are measured and a longer piece (Xq28 from the mother plus a far location of the crossed over gay male X DNA piece), or shorter DNA piece (a close or overlapped locations of the crossed over male X DNA pieces) can then be measured and compared in a linkage test.

Dr. Rice did a PCR analysis of the X chromosome and claimed that he did not find linkage in the Xq28 region, which, as you recall, is the site of the homosexuality inducing gene(s). However, Rice's interpretation of the results was challenged by Hamer who said that the data **does show** that a male crossed-over DNA in the Xq28 region is present and is responsible for homosexuality.

Method 5: Epigenetic changes of the DNA: Effect of Methylation. A scientist by the name of Tuck Ngun and his colleagues from the University of California (Los Angeles). Used this method to study heritable changes in gene expression that do not involve changes in the underlying DNA sequence. An epigenetic change is a phenotypic change without a change in genotype (a change in the DNA backbone). This change affects transcription - how the genes are translated into messenger RNAs. Epigenetic change is a regular and natural occurrence that is also influenced by several factors: age, the environment/lifestyle, and disease state. Epigenetic changes are of 3 types: Methylation, histone modification and gene silencing. DNA methylation, which was used by Ngun, causes the addition of methyl groups (CH3) in some places on the DNA backbone.

It was the study of Rice, which was described before in method 4, that inspired Tuck Ngun to examine epigenetic DNA methylation across the genomes of pairs of male twins. Identical twins have the same genetic backbone, but environmental factors lead to differences in how their DNA is methylated. In all, the study tested 37 pairs of twins in which one twin the pair was gay person, and the other was straight, and 10 pairs in which both twins were gay persons. The researchers tested over 400,000 data points in the DNAs of the twins to find methylations, to see how sexual orientation will affect methylation.

To sort through the methylation data, Ngun and his collaborators devised a machine-learning-algorithm called "Fuzzy Forest." They found methylations in nine regions, scattered across the genome, which could be used to predict a twin's gay orientation with a seventy percent accuracy. The researchers in Ngun's group have not stopped their studies with their published results and currently are testing the algorithm's accuracy in a more general population of men.

Method 6: WGS - Whole Genome Sequencing. This is a process of decoding the complete DNA sequence of an organism's genome. Whole genome-sequencing to find polymorphisms from SNP (a single nucleoside polymorphism) up to levels of polynucleotide- and whole genes' levels, had been used as a research tool. However, it is currently being introduced also to clinics to find harmful DNA mutations in all sorts of genetic diseases. In the past, it had been performed by very laborious procedures. However, nowadays, fluorescence-based sequencing methods with automatic DNA sequencers has become both easier, and several orders of magnitude faster.

The Whole Genome Sequencing of DNAs of people from the BioBank of Britain and from inventories of American citizens were performed after they had answered questions about their |sexual orientation. This was a study headed by the Finnish investigator Andrea Ganna and his colleagues from the Broad Institute of MIT. I had already described to you this excellent Finish investigator before. I am repeating it because of its importance.

Ganna and his collaborators performed a whole genome sequencing of the DNAs of half a million(!) heterosexuals, homosexuals, lesbians, and non-lesbians. This extensive study revealed five SNPs (Single nucleotide polymorphisms loci) that were significantly associated with same-sex preference. Two of the five polymorphisms were detected in both homosexuals and lesbians, two others in homosexuals alone, and one in lesbians only. In aggregate, all the discovered genetic polymorphisms accounted for 25% of homosexual or lesbian behavior. The study was revealing, but it should be noted that only SNPs were looked for, and not whole gene(s)' polymorphisms. Whole genes' polymorphisms could show an even clearer results in revealing the genes that induce gay or lesbian behavior. Interestingly, one male marker of the five genetic SNPs found in the Ganna study might be related to the sense of smell. This is a sense, that through pheromones, is involved in sexual attraction. What pheromones are, I shall explain to you in a minute.

I want you to note that Hamer himself thought that a man's sexual orientation depends only by about 30 percent on genes. Environmental factors also influence a man's sexual tendency. Environmental factors refer mostly to Hormones that affect the fetus in the womb. As a proof, there exist instances where one brother from a monozygotic pair of twins is gay, while the other is straight. Since they share identical DNA, if being gay person was solely determined by one's genes, then both twins should have been gay in every instance.

Hamer stressed that men were stamped with a homosexual preference already in the womb. There are a few cases in which **male** babies were operated on because of a medical necessity and were turned into girls. When they grew up, all of them were attracted to women and not to men. However, the best proof for biological factors that affect sexual tendency is the "Fraternal birth order effect" that I had already described to you earlier.

In this effect, the further late in the family a baby was born, that is he has more than 3 or 4 older siblings, the more he is prone to be gay. The proposed explanation for this phenomenon is that the mother becomes increasingly sensitized against the foreign material of the babies. She starts to produce antibodies against some important hormones that produces straight babies with the result that he is born homosexual.

Researchers analyzed blood and saliva samples from 409 pairs of brothers (including non-identical twins) over a period of five years, looking for shared locations of the genetic single nucleotide polymorphisms (SNPs). They found five SNPs commonly shared by the homosexual men, all clustered in two distinct locations on two separate chromosomes.

Alan Sanders, who led the study, said that the discovery "erodes the notion that sexual orientation is a choice". He cautioned that scientists have yet to zero in on which specific genes contribute to sexual orientation, stressing that complex traits like sexuality are the product of multiple environmental and genetic factors.

More scientists have hailed the find, which verifies a 1993 study by the US National Institutes of Health that was the first to show that same-sex activity was biologically decided as opposed a lifestyle choice.

"This study knocks another nail into the coffin of the 'chosen lifestyle' theory of Gay sexual behavior," neuroscientist Simon LeVay said. "Yes, we have a choice in life, to be ourselves or to conform to someone else's idea of normality, but being straight, bisexual, or gay, or none of these, is a central part of who we are, thanks in part to the DNA we were born with." A new study has quashed the idea that a single "gay gene" exists, scientists say. Instead, they found that gay behavior is influenced by a multitude of genetic variants each of which has a tiny effect. The researchers compare the situation to factors deciding a person's height, in which multiple genetic and environmental factors play roles.

The professor continued: "Dear Yohan, the studies that I described to you till now, highlight both the importance of the genetics as well as the complexity of the genetics, but note that genetics is not the whole story.

I had already described to you earlier the results of the Ganna study that used close to 500,000 individuals. In that study, about 4% of men and nearly 3% of women said that they had gay sexual experience. The team reported that they did not select the tested persons a-priori according to identity or orientation. By looking at sexual behavior and relatedness of individuals, they estimated that about a third of gay behavior is explained by genetics. That, they say, chimes with earlier twin studies that put the figure at about 30% to 50%.

Chapter 7:
Are genes the only key factors in producing gay persons?

Dr Brendan Zietsch, from the University of Queensland in Australia, one of the co-authors of the Ganna study said that it does not mean that the rest 70% of the gay behavior is due to upbringing or culture. He wrote that it is thought by many other scientists that non-genetic factors before birth, notably hormonal environment in the womb, also play a key role.

Hamer also commented on the Ganna research results and claimed that they provide yet another strand of evidence showing that there is a strong and significant genetic contribution to people's sexual behavior.

Unlike Hamer's work, the latest study does not assign any special importance to the X chromosome. The researchers say that this finding is not surprising, adding that the earlier findings would not meet today's bar for importance - they were based on a small sample size. Hammer also said he was not surprised by the results of the Ganna study – although he explained that scientists were looking at homosexual behavior, rather than at sexual orientation.

Qazi Rahman, a leading authority on sexual orientation research from King's College London, welcomed the study but said that the databases involved only obtained information from a small percentage of people who were invited to take part. That, he said, means that the genetic variants found in the research might reflect another trait characteristic to those who chose to respond."

Chapter 8:
Pheromones and homosexuality

Professor Hunter stopped talking for a few minutes after requesting permission from Yohan. Then he drank a soda and after wetting his palate and throat he asked: "Yohan, are we good till now? I bombed you with an extremely large amount of information!"

Yohan smiled and said: "Dear professor, do not worry on my account! I am digesting all that you teach me as any A student would. I did not inform you before that in college I majored in biology, and much later, I also took several master's degree courses in Genetics and several related subjects - physiology, biochemistry, immunology and even psychology and neurology. All these subjects gave me some inkling as to which type of scientists I should approach. Let me tell you that I am extremely impressed by your presentation, and I am very eager to see what you can suggest for the solution of my son's "problem."

Professor hunter was delighted, smiled, and said: "great! now I can increase my teaching tempo!" And then continued: "**Pheromones**! They are going to play a key role in my plan for treating of your son.

Now Yohan, tell me please, what is your son's name? Yohan's face lit up at the professor's question and he answered: "his name is Axel! as was my father's name…"

The professor then asked: "Yohan, don't be ashamed to tell me: Did you notice any deviant behavior in your father?" Yohan, paled somewhat, and answered: "Yes, I suspected that he liked men and not women, although he was married. He introduced several young "relatives" throughout his life into our family and never explained how they were related to us…" Professor hunter digested this information and continued with the pheromone subject:

"Humans, like many other species, are extremely sensitive to minute quantities of odors that are called "pheromones." When humans are near a male or a female who produces them, they will develop, according to their sexual orientations, a strong sexual desire and love for the pheromone-producing persons.

Since pheromones are produced in minute quantities, their study is beset with difficulty. There is a need for a complete cleanliness and lack of any extraneous odor in human test participants. Still, three classes of pheromones had been recognized: **axillary steroids, vaginal aliphatic acids, and pheromones that stimulate the vomeronasal organ.** What this organ is, I will soon describe to you.

Axillary steroids are produced by the testes, armpits (Sweat glands), the aureole and the nipples of the breast, eyelids, wings of the nostril, perianal region, and some parts of the external genitalia. Five axillary steroids have been discovered: Androstadiene, Androstadiennone, Androstanol, Androsterone and Androstenone. Their chemical formulas are known, and they have been synthesized by organic chemistry methods. The axillary steroids affect both females, gay people, and straight people. Each gender type is affected differently. Chemically synthesized axillary steroids are also commercially sold as aphrodisiacs.

The vaginal aliphatic acids are a class of volatile fatty acids that were first discovered in female Rhesus monkeys. The monkeys generate six types of these aliphatic acids in their vaginal secretions. These acids are also called "copulins." In humans, one-third of all women have all six types of copulins. These hormones are secreted near the presence of male semen. They become airborne and are transmitted to nearby males, thereby allowing the women to affect and even control the males through the hypothalamus. This class of pheromones is irrelevant to the first stage of our research, since they affect only straight men.

A Swedish Research showed that when both gay persons and straight women populations are exposed to the testosterone derivative Androsterone [it is also classified as one of the five axillary steroids, that I mentioned a second ago], they respond with a sexual excitation in the thalamus, as shown by an fMRI study.

Because pheromones can increase attractiveness and lead to a better sex life, fragrance and cosmetics companies have been working to bottle the scent of pheromones like androsterone into perfumes. Studies using pheromones at the University of Chicago showed that men who used topical pheromones, had a 52% improvement in starting conversations and an even better rate of improvement in <u>staying engaged</u> in conversation. They also saw improvement in getting compliments, noticeable flirting from the opposite sex and a 40% increase in female sexual responsiveness.

In the same study, women who used the synthetic pheromones found themselves asked on dates more often and an increase in foreplay during sexual activity. 74% of the women who participated in the study saw a huge increase in their interactions with men overall, with most reported having sex more often and receiving more intimacy such as hugs and cuddling after a sexual act. Another study in 2002 by San Francisco State University showed that women who "wore" synthetic pheromones were found to be more attractive by their partners.

Straight men, have an fMRI response, to a second pheromone – an estrogen-like compound found in women's urine. The conclusion of the study was that sexual attraction, whether same-sex or opposite-sex-oriented, operates similarly on a biological level.

All pheromones affect the hypothalamus that is situated in the limbic system of the brain. the limbic system is a set of brain structures found on both sides of the thalamus and primarily support a variety of functions including emotion, behavior, motivation, long-term memory, and the sense of smell. "Emotional life" is housed in the limbic system, and it aids the formation of memories.

Let me now describe to you the structure of the Limbic System: The Limbic system is a set of brain structures found on both sides of the thalamus immediately beneath the medial temporal lobe of the Cerebellum. It supports a variety of functions that I had already described to you a few seconds ago.

The major parts of the Limbic System are as follows: **The Thalamus** is a part of the brain that handles detecting and relaying information from our senses of smell and vision. The Thalamus is found within the brainstem and is part of the information pathway that goes into the Cerebrum. The cerebrum is the section of the brain that handles thinking and movement.

The **hypothalamus** is a vital part of the Limbic System that responds to hormones and also produces hormones. These hormones control water levels in the body, sleep cycles, body temperature and food intake. The hypothalamus is found beneath the Thalamus, (and that explains its name).

The **Cingulate Gyrus** serves as a pathway that transmits messages between the inner and outer portions of the limbic system.

The **Amygdalae** are a pair of almond-shaped clusters of nerve cells in the temporal lobe of the cerebrum. The amygdalae are responsible for preparing the body for emergency situations, such as being 'startled,' and for storing memories of events for future recognition.

The Amygdalae also aid in the development of memories, particularly those related to emotional events and emergencies. They are also specifically involved with the development of the fear-emotion and can be the cause of extreme expressions of fear, as in the case of panic. Additionally, the Amygdalae play a key role in pleasure and **sexual arousal** and may vary in size depending on the sexual activity and maturity of the individual.

There are several "way-stations" through which an odor, including pheromones or their resulting electrical stimulus, move to excite the brain centers. In 1991, Richard Axel of the Howard Hughes Medical Institute, and Linda Buck at the Fred Hutchinson Cancer Research Center gave us the first inkling of how we smell and received for that a Nobel Prize. They discovered about 1,000 genes that encode for olfactory (smelling) **receptors** inside the human nose and found that each receptor is tuned for only a small number of odors.

When we smell something, the air is sucked up into our nostrils over a bony ridge called <u>turbinate</u> which adds more surface area to our nose. Here the air travels over millions of olfactory **receptor neurons** that sit on a stamp-sized tissue called the "olfactory epithelium" or also the "olfactory mucosa". This tissue exists on the turbinates that are on the roof of the nasal cavity and the odor molecules in the air stimulate the receptors that are on it.

The smelling, more so than any other sense, is also intimately linked to the parts of the brain that process emotion and associative learning. The olfactory bulb in the brain, which is the first waystation that sorts sensation into perception, is part of an added waystation which is the limbic system with its amygdala and hippocampus. These structures are vital to our memory as well as the memory of thousands of smells." The professor here concluded his exposition by saying: "Yohan, our target for a conversion of Axel is going to be Pheromones and their action in smelling.

More specifically we are going to target an organ in the nose that is called the Vomeronasal Organ (short name VMO). It interacts with the important third group of pheromones that I described earlier. The interaction is via **receptors** on the turbinates that are part of the VMO. The **receptors** are a group of eight G-protein-coupled receptors called: V1R, TAR, TAAR5, TAAR6, TAAR8, TAAR9, V2R, and FPR. (G-proteins are wide-spread types of proteins in the body that act as molecular switches). Each pheromone odor sets off an electrical signal in the receptors, although the exact identities of the receptor or group of receptors is still unknown. My plan for the first stage of the conversion of Axel is to find the receptor or receptors that transfer the electrical signal for homosexuality.

The professor stopped his narration, drank some water, and waited for Yohan's response to his plan. Yohan reflected for a minute and then said: "Jack! I am extremely impresses with your plan! Tell me please, will a 100 million dollars suffice for your work, at least for the next year?"

When Jack heard the sum that Yohan was going to contribute, he opened his mouth in surprise, and for a minute or two forgot to close it. when he could speak again, he said: "Yohan, this is more than enough! I shall be able to return most of it at the end of the first year after we convert Axel!

Yohan was happy with Professor Hunter's reaction and with his optimism and said: "Jack, don't worry about returning the money! The project is important to both of us and to Axel, and I want to ensure that no lack of money should hinder its progress.! How shall I transfer the money to you?"

Professor Hunter said: "Yohan, I am extremely impressed with the sum, and I am incredibly happy, for it will enable me to perform an extensive study with a large team on a problem, that really intrigues me and all psychologists and, most importantly, may help your son. I shall be able now to hire plenty of scientists to help me with disciplines with which I am less familiar.

As for the transfer of the money, here is what I suggest: Berkeley had long received endowments from private foundations and alumni. Notable among the donors were Mark Zuckerberg, the Bill and Melinda Gates Foundation, the Israeli-Russian billionaire Yuri Milner, and many others. Also, over the years," Hunter added, "anonymous donors had donated many millions of dollars to the Science and Engineering school, to which I belong, including a 2009 gift of $100 million to support the department of molecular engineering, and a $70-million gift in 2019 to support the Life Science Incubator known as the Ingenuity Hub"...

"Most importantly," Jack continued, "The Board of Regents of Berkeley created in 2014 a fund that would supply venture capital to support start-up companies of students and faculty. I believe that we can fit into this fund. It will mean a donation from you to the Psychology department for the development of a start-up company. I shall put you in touch with the Board of Regents and you will say that you want to support a start-up venture within the premises of the psychology department that will be managed by me as the chief investigator of the company and its CEO.

I shall also tell the regents that our start-up will modernize the Psychology department since I intend to equip it with the most modern analytical and synthesizing machines that will be used by both the start-up company and the department's personnel. Our start-up shall be called "Gay sexual behavior and Science."

Its vision will be to develop drugs or technologies intended to convert gay people to heterosexuality. If we shall succeed, the drug or technology will be available to all gay people who would wish to convert. This way, your donation will become a start-up support, and will give us an exemption from tax deduction.

Now, Yohan, with your permission, as chief investigator and CEO of the start-up company, I would like to draw a salary of 960,000 dollars per year. I am close to retirement and, instead of retiring and living further on my pension, I shall have to spend many hours per day with my scientists in the lab and conference room. Besides, I shall have to resign from my post in the University and will lose both my salary and my pension. Therefore, I think that my proposition of such a salary is reasonable. Is this OK with you?"

Donner said: "Jack, why you ask? The money is yours to do whatever you want with it, including the salary which you certainly deserve. You are asking much less than even the most junior of my managers."

Only now, with Donner's last remark, the realization of his new position as the CEO of a rich start-up company reached Hunter's awareness. He was struck speechless with the vistas of the scientific research possibilities that the money opened.

Then, happily, Professor Hunter said: "Well, Yohan, how does my tax evasion plan strike you?" Donner said: "Why, I can only say "Wow," as the saying goes! I like your idea very much! I was a bit angry, not at you, God forbid. I thought that if I assigned the money to you as a gift, we shall have to pay a large chunk of it to the Income Tax! In truth, I could have compensated for this tax deduction by increasing my donation. I hope that our start-up, if it succeeds, may help thousands of currently persecuted gay people. Therefore, we are justified to "cheat" the Government. Their strongboxes are full as it is with tax money, and I help to fill them even more every year with my tax return..." Both men laughed and shook hands, happy that they succeeded to pull one over the government's head.

Donner ordered a snack and wine to celebrate the launching of their start-up company. Then about half an hour later, he arranged Hunter's voyage home. They decided on a reporting method to let Donner know how the establishment of the start-up company is progressing, and, more importantly, how its research is progressing.

Hunter's travel home was uneventful, but he could not relax. His mind was all afire going over his meeting with Donner, the large research donation, their new start-up, his plans for research, and more. Finally, he asked the free pilot for a bottle of champagne to continue his earlier celebration with Donner. But more so, to calm his nerves before he would blow a fuse or a gasket or both because of his excitement and happiness.

After Donner's announcement on the size of his endowment and his approval of a salary, Hunter went to the bathroom to "wash his hands." Then, using his mobile phone, he jubilantly talked with Flora, reporting to her the happy news. Also, he did not forget to mention that their household budget is going to increase greatly and that they will be able to support their sons in their colleges, especially Jack Junior. Jack Junior has a small girl to support, and his wife worked overtime to make ends meet. Flora was overjoyed, but, in addition, she could not refrain from the temptation to tell Hunter not to forget to whom he owes thanks for his new position...

Chapter 9:
The Scientists of the start-up company

Since Professor Hunter now had unlimited funds, he at once, started to make clever use of it. He began to activate his plan to gather young post-docs whose pH, D. theses and their current post-doctorals or residency training are in the areas that he assumed that he needed to employ. He decided that these areas ought to be Immunochemistry, molecular Genetics, Organic/Protein Chemistries and Pharmacology. He also intended to hire one resident from an Ear nose and throat (ENT) clinic.

He hoped to receive many applications from post-docs who will be attracted by his offer to double the average post-docs' salary. He also planned to offer his scientists relocation expenses as well as added excellent social benefits. He even decided to include free dental insurance plans for the post-docs and their families.

The only limiting stipulation that he was going to impose on his future employees was to sign an NDA (Non-Disclosure Agreement) form. This is a common document that start-up companies or existing companies use to prevent their personnel from leaking out the secrets of companies and to prevent post-docs from the publishing of papers of the companies' interim findings.

This was needed because post-doctoral fellows are very keen to publish scientific papers to advance to tenure positions in major universities or research institutions.

Professor Hunter liked to work with post-docs. Because of their need to succeed, they worked very diligently. Below is the ad that the professor composed. Among other temptations, it also held a notice of the high salaries for the candidates.

The Professor published the ad in the most prestigious journals which also had the largest distribution among scientific circles.

"A call to hire post-doctoral fellows and medical interns for a new start-up company, which is headed by a well-known Psychology Professor. The company will operate within the premises of the Psychology Department of the University of California (Berkley). The company will study technics that will deal with an important aspect of human life.

Wanted are post-doctoral fellows who are currently specializing or had completed their training in the following areas: Immuno-chemistry, Molecular Genetics, Organic Chemistry plus Protein Chemistry, and pharmacology. Wanted is also a medical resident in an Ear, Nose, and throat (ENT) residency.

Applicants who will be accepted, will receive a salary that is double that of the current average salaries of post-Docs and residents. They will also receive excellent fringe benefits. Interested applicants are requested to send their CV, list of publications and a description of their experience by E-mail to JH.psy@AOL.

Only suitable applicants shall be invited to an interview. Sorry, negative answers will they not be sent!

Professor J. Hunter, University of California (Berkley)

The professor received many applications from post-docs who were drawn by the excellent salary offered by the professor. Also, the fact that the professor did not mention the name or names of the projects of the startup, attracted other applicants. It was quite rare for a psychologist to obtain grants to set up what looked like a rich start-up unless it was supported by the military. Therefore, some post-docs were attracted by what they thought that Professor

Hunter planned to study. Was it a military hush-hush project in which they can excel and obtain a tenure position as government employees or in the military??

Others did not care on what they are going to work if their paychecks kept coming. When they started their careers, grants were plentiful in all areas. But now, unemployment ran amok… The unemployment was the direct effect of the Coronavirus that attacked various locations in the country, many of which had campuses of major universities that closed. The Coronavirus also dealt the economy of the country a fatal blow, so that some applicants were without any means of subsistence whatsoever.

Also, some "smart" applicants saw the list of the available jobs for the startup and realized that it was a project with important medical applications. Perhaps even a project to develop a vaccine against the terrible Coronavirus in addition to the existing ones of Pfizer, etc.?… If so, why put a professor of psychology and not an immunologist or a biochemist in charge of the start-up?

Whatever the reason was, Professor Hunter received over 80 applications from excellent post-docs. He had to spend many hours to select the best applicants. He felt like farmer who had several choice agricultural lots and had to decide which of them to seed or plant and which of them to leave fallow so that they will renew their bacteria, and earthworm populations for the next year…

Finally, after exceptionally long deliberations, he chose nine scientists and printed their names in a table for the sake of future study. He printed their names, and other key details such as experience in work with Gender problems, and so on. From time to time, he removed one name and put in another name instead, that seemed to him to be more suitable for the moment. Professor Hunter had a bad case of inability to decide, in the face of too many riches... In his past scientific career, he never had that many applicants.

Following below is the list of all the suitable applicants that the professor compiled:

Name of scientist	Scientific aera	Experience in gender studies	Years post doc'ing	Degree of suitability
Jerry Oren	Organic Chemistry Protein Chemistry	NO	3	9
Josh Kell	Organic Chemistry Protein Chemistry	NO	3	9
Ayala Gibbons	Immuno-Chemistry	NO	3	9
Jane Erlanger	Immuno-Chemistry	NO	3	9
Bernardo Ban	Molecular and Genetic Biology	NO	3	9
Jim Scuole	Molecular and Genetic Biology	NO	3	9
Jill Wild	Pharmacology	YES	3	9
Amanda Shor	Pharmacology	YES	3	9
June Meers	ENT	YES	3	9

To help in the running of the start-up company, professor hunter hired an elderly executive secretary with plenty of experience. She arranged an extensive communication center for him that would also allow the scientists to conduct both private and scientific communications with the entire world.

At Hunter's request, Mary invited all the selected scientists to the same day to have an orientation meeting. He was in a position in which he did not have to choose between many final applicants. Both the two immuno-chemists, the two molecular geneticists, and the two Organic/Protein chemists were obviously excellent scientists. He also did not have to choose between two ENT residents, since the final table had just one applicant. However, he did have to choose one pharmacologist out of two applicants.

Before his selection interview with the two pharmacologists, Professor Hunter met the ENT resident plus the six selected post-docs for a very short welcome meeting. He told them that he will meet the whole team to discuss their company's future research once the single pharmacologist was chosen.

The three women post-docs, Ayala, Jill, and June were about 30 years of age and according to their CVs, unmarried. The two immunochemists, and the two molecular geneticists were nearer to Thirty-five years of age. Three of them were married, out of which two had one child.

Now Professor Hunter had to choose one postdoc from among two pharmacologists. He devised a questionnaire for their selection interviews. He was mostly interested to find out what is their forte in research might be, and how proficient they were in their specialties.

Below is the questionnaire that he used in the interview.

At the start of the "test," the professor first met Jill Wild and said:

"Hi Jill, I am really pleased to meet you. You are the first candidate that I am interviewing from among two applicants of the very final stage. I am going to give you a typed questionnaire that you will have to answer concisely. You have one hour for your answers. I do not require you to answer all the questions. Whatever you will succeed to answer is fine!

Following is the list of questions that the professor devised:

* Question 1: Are you proficient in the various technics of drug synthesis?

* Question 2: Please describe the production of any imaginary new drug that you choose, and describe for it how you would devise for it the following parameters:

* Question 3: Manufacturing Process of the drug substance and the drug product,

* Question 4: The excipients that you would add to the drug substance to turn it to a drug product,

* Question 5: The In-Process Controls of the production procedures of the drug substance and drug product,

* Question 6: The sterilization procedure of the drug product,

* Question 7: What microbial limits you would set for the drug substance and drug product?

* Question 8: What analytical Procedures and Microbiological procedures would you use to test the raw materials?

* Question 9: Describe the manufacturing facility, the production instruments and testing site of the imaginary new drug that you chose to synthesize.

* Question 10: Are you capable of working with a computer program that will design and visualize high affinity blockers to various proteins and carbohydrates?

* Question 11: Do you have experience in the operation of a mass spectrometer and a LCMS? I bought them at the recommendation of a chemist who said that my chemists and pharmacologists would need them for their analytical work."

Jill answered the questions to the best of her ability. Professor Hunter read the answers and said: "Thank you Jill for your answers. I shall make my decision after I have read the answers of the other applicant."

The results of both tests, when Professor Hunter read them, presented a problem: Both pharmacologist applicants seemed highly qualified, and Professor Hunter could not decide which of them to choose. Finally, he decided to choose them by lottery. He put 2 tags in a hat and let each of the contestant pick one, and Jill Wild won.

He regretfully compensated the unlucky applicant, Amanda Shor, handsomely for her time and travel expenses and parted apologetically from her.

Chapter 10:
The professor describes the project of the start-up company

After the selection interviews were over, Professor Hunter told his secretary, Mary Merriwether, to invite his new colleagues to Berkley. When all have them finally arrived, he gave them a grand tour of his/their new "kingdom", of which he was enormously proud. He also let them choose places in the 2 labs that the start-up hired from the. department. These were empty but equipped labs that their near-retirement professors still sentimentally held but did not use any more.

The professor also hired an excellent cook, Jane Perl, which was going to supply all the scientists with meals and light snacks at all hours when they worked, at least ten hours per each day, including Friday.

Then the professor invited his new colleagues to the conference room for a description of their research subject. At the conference room each of the scientists introduced himself and described briefly his or her specialization, past experiences, and the universities in which he/she was trained for his/her graduate degrees. The professor now was ready to present the project on which the new colleagues will work on with him.

But before Hunter's description of the project, the scientists mingled together and became more acquainted with each other.

They also got a taste of Perl's snacks and then went for a long briefing concerning their future research subject.

All of Professor hunter's scientists finally entered the Department's conference hall. At long last, Professor Hunter could get to the practical details: the description of the start-ups project.

The professor started:

"Before I shall start to describe our project, I want to describe to you what goodies I am going to throw your way. Well, in addition to your high salary, 100,000$ per year, the company will pay all your relocation expenses:

1. The cost of a house-finding trip. The company will cover all your back and forth travelling costs and that of your companions, wives, and boy-friends for that.
2. Payment of all your rent and utility fees for all the time that we shall work together in the company.
3. The company will pay all the costs of movers who will pack up your household goods and transport them to your new homes.
4. The company will also pay all your dental bills and those of your family and girl/boy-friends.
5, The company will pay all your contract-breaking fines for your current homes. As you can see, I try to achieve a situation in which nothing will distract you from doing an excellent job."

Dr. George Erlanger looked around and saw that his all colleagues exuded great satisfaction with their employment terms and therefore he felt justified to express thanks also for his colleagues, and said: "Boss, I think that I shall not err if I'll speak for all of us here and say "Many thanks! We shall do everything in our power to succeed." All the other postdocs nodded their heads happily and spontaneously began to applaud!

Professor Hunter, with a keen eye, noticed during the meeting that all the participating women were pretty and sexy. The thought crossed his mind that it might be worth to test their sexual mores… But then the professor drove this thought away and started his first long briefing:

"I am glad to meet all of you and hope that we shall work well together. You have been selected out of many applicants because you meet the requirement of our start-up venture. Our start-up is intended to develop a technic or a drug for the conversion of the sexual orientation of homosexual persons to heterosexuality. Our sponsor, who is generously financing our start-up, is an intelligent evangelist and oil-magnate from Oklahoma. by the name of Yohan Donner. He has an only son who is also an evangelist that he wants to convert with the son's willing cooperation. He is pouring a lot of money into our venture, since he believes that there are also other gay people like his son who do not feel comfortable with their sexual orientation or live in countries where their sexual orientation endangers them. Therefore, they are apt to lose their lives if they are caught." When the professor finally described the nature of the start-up's project, a hush fell in the lab and all the scientists started to digest the news.

The professor continued: "As you know, the sexual orientation of a man is decided in his mother's womb and is not the result of a learned, willful depravity. Several genes and prenatal hormones decree his sexual reference when he will mature. This fact is a common knowledge. However, our sponsor is a devout evangelist and so is his son. The homosexual son wants to follow the New Testament's directives against 'Sodomy', and his father helps him in this quest.

Our subject, besides being important to our sponsor and his son, is also important to many psychologists who study gender preferences. Moreover, and primarily, our project is important to the future of the USA and the world for the following reason:

There are various surveys that were carried out by several poling methods and by important institutions to figure out the extent of homosexuality and lesbianism in the USA. They produced a variety of results, but most of them produced frequency results of 3.5% up to 5%. This is not such a high percentage; however, this number is slowly rising.

We shall eventually come to a situation in which the third genders, and especially homosexual persons, may be in danger from racists! A reaction to their spreading may start by many American bigots and racists, which hate anybody who is "different." As a result, gay people may be in grave danger and will be persecuted just as Black people were and still are! Therefore, there may be many gay people who may want to convert to heterosexuality and thus escape persecution. If we succeed in our project, we shall be fulfilling an important social and democratic function. If we fail, the US may be, eventually, torn apart by a terrible civil strife. This is a bleak evolutionary outcome that our government should study and prevent.

The increase in the numbers of gays in the world, albeit a slow one, happens because of the following reasons:

1. The gay population will increase through births of gay babies due to heritable mutations in the DNA of straight persons.

2. An important increase also happens a result of the "Fraternal birth order" effect. In this effect, the more preceding grown-up brothers a baby has, the greater is the chance that he may be born gay:

   Every grown-up brother in the family increases by 33% the chance that the newborn small baby will be gay. The best hypothesis to explain this phenomenon is that the immune system of the mother becomes more active immunologically during her pregnancies with each next birth and produces antibodies against some important heterosexuality-inducing proteins. That is because her immune system considers her fetuses to be foreign to her body.

3. Birth of gay babies because of crossing-over during the process of the meiosis process that is intended to produce male sperm and female ovum.

4. Additionally, ever since the development of in-vitro fertilization (IVF) and surrogate motherhood, and even before that, many gay people felt a primal urge to procreate and transfer their genes to posterity. They father children by donating their own sperm to surrogate mothers, or to an ovum in a petri dish (IVF), by simple injection with a syringe… It is not known if any or many or all the newborn babies from such an IVF with surrogate motherhood encounter will be homosexual. This is because the procreation wish of gay "fathers" is still too recent and have not been reported in population assessments. However, the chances are that their progeny will be also gay when they grow up!

It is true that males, gay or heterosexual, donate during fertilization a complement of chromatids with a Y chromatid only, and Gay sexual behavior genes pass by an X chromatid. However, as the result of a crossing-over, a crossed-over X of the female may hold a gay X piece from the male! In addition, the X chromatid of chromosome 8 may transfer another gay marker. Therefore, we do not work for Donner and his son alone, but also for the future of the USA and every other place in the world where racism is rampant!!!

I should have written in my hiring ad what our project is going to be, but on purpose I did no.t Perhaps you had visions of work on a "cure for cancer" or some other important subject. Also, I was afraid that some of you may disdain working on our project, before hearing me out. In the case of such disdain, I can hire other postdocs instead. But, believe me, the project is a part of real life, and it is a worth-while one, especially for the future of democratic, egalitarian, humane societies. I shall bid now goodbye to those who will not work with me on the project without any hard feelings, and I shall also finance all his/her travel expenses to Berkley and back home. I shall give you now a few minutes to think about your decision. Please raise your hand if you do not want the job.

The Professor waited some minutes, and no one raised his hand. With gratification he continued: "as is the rule in all start-up companies, all of us will have to postpone the publishing of papers on interesting interim findings that may materialize during our studies. I know that you must publish to obtain academic positions in major universities or in research institutions after your stint in our startup. However, to the best of my knowledge, no one is competing with us, so that we are not in a hurry to publish. If, and when, we shall succeed, you and I will publish a big, important paper as a team. The names of the authors on the paper will be written by an alphabetical order. Now, as is the rule in start-up companies, you will have to sign a document called NDA – "non-disclosure agreement" whose purpose is to prevent leaks of the company's results."

Then, as if on cue, Mary came with the non-disclosure forms for the post-docs to sign.

The Professor finished everything that he planned to say and added: "That is all for today. Return to your homes and arrange all your relocation businesses and return quickly to our business!"

On the next day, all the scientists either flew, or drove to their homes to leave their old jobs and specializations and bid their professors or bosses and colleagues goodbye. Before leaving for home to get movers to pack and transport their household effects and furniture, all the scientists rented apartments in Berkley. For this purpose, they were, aided by a large real estate company that Mary, the secretary of the company, recommended. Since she lived in Berkley all her life, she also helped the scientists in their searches. The wives or girl/boy friends of the scientists participated in the choosing of their new apartments through videos that they viewed in "real time."

Luckily, all the scientists lived in rented apartments and parted amicable from their property owners after paying a penalty for breaking the lease. They paid the penalty without any compunction since they were rapidly compensated for it by the company. They also received generous checks for all their expenses from an accountant by the name of Bill Cameron that Hunter hired. All the scientists were quickly packed at their homes for transit to their new homes, and flew or drove back to Berkley, ready to start their work.

When the last scientist had finally come back to the start-up, Professor Hunter assembled all of them again in the conference room and began to delineate the strategy of their future work.

He said: "Dear colleagues, I hope that all of you are already settled comfortably in your new homes. If there is any problem, whether small or large, please consult Mary, our company's secretary who had lived all her life in the city and she will help you with everything that you may need. She can also recommend good schools for children that you may have legally or illegitimately bred. Hah! Hah!"

"Now I would like to describe the work that we shall perform. I want to start by describing to you research conducted in Sweden: Swedish scientists have found that gay people and straight women responded to an odor (pheromone) that they were given to smell. After they smelled it, they responded with a sexual arousal. This was a testosterone derivative found in men's sweat which is called Androsterone.

Upon sexual arousal, a region in the hypothalamus was activated, as shown by an fMRI study. To those who do not know: fMRI is functional Magnetic Resonance Imaging. It measures brain activity by detecting Changes in blood flow in the brain.

Straight men, on the other hand, had a similar fMRI response (sexual arousal) to a second pheromone - an estrogen-like compound found in women's urine. The conclusion is that arousal and sexual attraction, whether same-sex or opposite-sex oriented, runs with pheromones as mediators. We are going to concentrate on pheromone receptors that exist I the nose as targets for a conversion. But first I need to describe to you how odors, in general, are sensed and recorded by the brain. Some of you are familiar with what I am going to say but bear with me".

"There are several "waystations" through which an odor, or its resulting electrical stimulus, moves to excite the brain centers. In 1991, Richard Axel of the Howard Hughes Medical Institute and Linda Buck at the Fred Hutchinson Cancer Research Center gave us the first inkling of how we smell and received for it a Nobel Prize. They discovered about 1,000 genes that encode for olfactory receptors inside the human nose and found that each receptor is tuned for only a small number of odors.

When we smell something, the air is sucked up into our nostrils over bony ridges called "turbinates" which add more surface area in our noses. Here the air travels over millions of olfactory receptor neurons that sit on a stamp-sized tissue called the "olfactory epithelium" or also the "olfactory mucosa." This tissue exists on turbinates that are situated the roof of the nasal cavity and the odor molecules in the air stimulate the receptors that are in it.

Smelling, more so than any other sense, is also intimately linked to the parts of the brain that process emotion and associative learning. The olfactory bulb in the brain, which is the first waystation that sorts sensation into perception, is part of an additional waystation called the limbic system - a system that includes the amygdala and hippocampus. These structures are vital to our behavior, mood, and memory as well as the memory of thousands of odors.

Chapter 11:
The wonderful Vomeronasal organ

Some pheromones, however, are smelled differently from what I just told you. They are smelled through an organ called the Vomeronasal Organ (VMO) that is present in the soft tissue of the nasal epithelium and slowly disappears during growth, to leave only a vestigial organ. This organ is important in sexual excitation since it responds with great sensitivity to pheromones. Most investigators tried to find the VMO in holes of the palate, and not in the nasal epithelial structure, because the VMO was vestigial. It slowly degenerates during a baby's life. However, in a high microscopic magnification study, a scientist, Dr. Win, found in 2015 evidence of VMO's in 13 of his 22 tested cadavers (59.1%) and in 22 of his 78 living patients (28.2%). Also, in a study published in 2016, Stoyanov and associates found VMOs in 26.83% of the Bulgarian population. They used retrospective microscopic analyses of a thousand nasal endoscopies (nasal scrape samples) of outpatients that were stored in an archive.

The VMO interacts with the stimulating pheromones via receptors that are present on it. The receptors are a group of eight G-protein-coupled receptors that are called: V1R, TAR, TAAR5, TAAR6, TAAR8, TAAR9, V2R, and FPR. G-proteins are wide-spread types of proteins in the body that act as molecular switches.

Each pheromone odor sets off a signal in the receptors, although the identity of the receptor or group of receptors that are "pinged" by a given pheromone is still unknown.

We shall try to unlock this mystery as I shall describe later and may get a nice feather in our caps by way of a beautiful, published paper. An electrical signal that is induced by the pheromones travels along the receptors and their olfactory nerves in the Vomeronasal Organ and from there to the amygdala and the hippocampus.

The reason that I concentrate so much on the sense of smell is because the eight G-protein VMO receptors are going to be our first target for action. Luckily, past work by a protein chemist by the name of Correli in 2012 supplied us with the sequences of the amino acids that make up the 8 G-Protein VMO receptors. These sequences can be found in one of the amino acids sequence databases that is called FASTA. Correli deposited the sequences, as is the custom for scientists, in the free internet. Files in the FASTA format hold information about the kinds of amino acids of many proteins. These sequences are divided among smaller databases whose names are Uniprot, Sprot and Protein Data Bank (PDB). According to Corelli's results, three of the eight receptors are short polypeptides that have 7, 9, and 10 amino acids, respectively. The 5 other receptors have between 19 and 22 amino acids. My plan of attack would be to "paralyze" the VMO receptors, one at a time, or in groups, <u>with antibodies specific against each receptor</u> to see if the "paralysis" will "turn-off" gay subjects' lust for men. The gay candidates tested will be, of course, well paid for their agreement to serve as a subject for experimentation. Besides, after each experiment the subjects will be reversed to their original condition.

We shall apply the blocking antibody(ies) diluted in nasal washes so that they will react with each chosen receptor. Then we shall screen to them pornographic movies of gay people making love. Before the screening we shall attach to their penises a blood flow manometer. IF they will get "excited" by the movies, their penises will swell with blood or still will be flaccid (empty, indifferent). The effect of the specific antibodies against each receptor is reversible, since after the testing of the effect of each antibody, we shall rinse the subject's nose with a mild acidic nasal wash. The acid will dissociate the antibody from each receptor without harming its activity. This way we shall test each of the single 8 receptors, or groups of receptors.

How shall we get antibodies specific for each of the receptors? Well, based on Corelli's work, we will ask Jerry and Josh, our chemists to synthesize each polypeptide receptor. They will do it with the help of our mute and deaf friend - the 'Biotage' automatic peptide synthesizer.

Then, we will ask Ayala Gibbons and Armand Erlanger, or Jerry and Josh, to bind each of the peptide receptors, to Bovine Serum Albumin (BSA, the albumin from bovine blood) and inject the receptor-BSA molecules into rabbits to produce antibodies.

The peptides alone are too small and cannot serve as antigens by themselves. However, in the covalent combination with BSA, the rabbits will produce both anti-BSA and ant-receptor antibodies. Then, Ayala and Armand will bind BSA to an insoluble powdered plastic matrix and load it into columns. They will pass each rabbit antiserum through these BSA columns. The various unnecessary anti-BSA antibodies (IgG, IgM, etc.) will bind to the column, while out of the column will flow pure anti peptide-receptor antibodies.

The immunization of the rabbits will take about 3 months and, unfortunately, cannot be hurried. We shall check the pace of the antibody production by a test called ELISA (short for Enzyme Linked Immunosorbent Assay). The ELISA uses 8x12 rows of wells (small cylinders) that exist inside a plastic block that is made of Maleic Anhydride Activated Plastic. This material allows immediate strong attachment (absorption) of amine-containing peptides, such as our 8 peptide receptors, to the microplate wells. Then we shall apply consecutive 1:2 dilutions of the various rabbit anti receptor antibodies to the wells and allow them to bind to the various peptide receptors in the wells. If the rabbits have already produced anti receptor antibodies, after the washing of the unbound antibodies from the plate, we shall detect the bound rabbit antibodies in the wells (if any) with an anti-rabbit antibody that has a staining enzyme attached to it for detection. The antibody-enzyme complex will be detected with a staining substrate. The last still-reacting 1:2 dilution of the rabbit antiserum will give us the "'titer" (strength) of the anti-receptor rabbit antibody.

After isolating the pure anti-receptor antibodies from the above columns, each of them will be tested singly or in groups in the noses of our volunteer gay person subjects. Now I want to address my immuno-chemists! Am I right in my description of the production of pure anti receptor antibodies?" Surprised at the accurate description of the production of the rabbit anti-receptor antibodies method, the two immuno-chemists nodded their heads in confirmation. As a result, all the postdocs applauded heartily!

Professor Hunter smiled happily since he had proved to his team that he is also a good scientist and not just a CEO with a control of the moneybag. What his team did not know was that he worked summers as a student lab-technician in a commercial antibody-producing-company: injecting rabbits with various antigens, bleeding them and testing their presence and strengths (antibody titer) in all sorts of ELISA tests ...

Professor Hunter then said: "now I want you to think deeply and try to come out with a plan of your own. If it makes good sense, we shall perform it in addition to the blocking rabbit anti- receptor antibodies." The scientists sat quietly trying to produce an idea of their own. Then Armand Ban hesitantly raised his hand, and Professor Hunter said: "good, Armand, let's hear your idea".

Armand said: "No Professor, I don't have any additional idea. I am willing to volunteer as a gay person that I am to do the job of trying the excitation of my penis with the paid gay person candidates, but without any pay... Here I am coming out of the closet, willingly, for us. I won't have to wear a blood flow measuring instrument on my penis since I shall report to you my own exact penis-responses."

Professor Hunter was not overly surprised at Armand's confession. His long past studies with gay people had already prepared him in advance for Armand's eventually coming out of the closet. Therefore, he underhandedly said: "Good. Then that settles it", to show that he does not want any remarks on the matter. Armand's colleagues also refrained from any comments and the matter dissipated itself.

Chapter 12:
Jill suggests an additional project to obtain a conversion

Then the pharmacologist Jill Willd, raised her hand and said: "Professor, I think I have an idea". The professor said: "good, Jill, shoot!"

Jill thought a bit and then said: "As you all know, more and more new drugs are introduced as treatment options for diseases by the pharmaceutical industry because of the need to replace less optimal drugs, and the problem of Drug Resistant Bacteria. As a result, the incidence and prevalence of medication-induced side-effects of drugs continues to escalate. Many drugs can cause partial Anosmia (loss of the sense of smell). Let me enumerate some of the drugs that I can remember, offhand, that cause partial Anosmia: Antibiotics such as Amoxicillin and Ciprofloxacin; Antihistamines such as Prednisone and Fluticasone; High blood pressure controlling drugs: Enalapril; Anti blood lipids such as, Levastatin, Psycho-pharmacologic drugs as Citalopram, Fluoxetine, and sertraline.

"Professor, if it sounds right to you, I suggest that Armand and I shall each pick all drugs sequentially and modify them chemically into several similar molecules in the hope that the changed drugs will cause a <u>complete anosmia</u> instead of just a <u>partial one</u>. Anosmia is caused by inflammation of the nasal mucosa followed by the blockage of nasal passages. The inflammation is due to a chronic mucosal swelling in the lining of the paranasal sinus and in the middle and above the turbinates.

A good thing with this idea is that the olfactory function returns to normal in few days after drug stoppage. But this method may take much more time than your idea. The subjects will require longer time to recuperate."

Professor Hunter reflected a few seconds and then said: "Jill, I like your idea. You and Armand can start at once. I tried to equip the chemistry lab for you. To save time, I bought for you an excess of glassware such as Crucibles, Retorts, Mortars and Pestles, Erlenmeyers, Beakers, Volumetric Flasks, Test Tubes, Boiling Flasks, Ovens and much more Paraphernalia of your trade. For that I was given directions from an organic chemist in Berkley.

I did not buy any chemicals for you since I realize that you must order chemicals yourself according to your own needs. I think that you have already seen that your labs are fully equipped. The Organic/protein chemists' labs also hold all sorts of glassware and hardware plus computers, but they are also without chemicals. Once your labs will be stocked with the necessary reactants, reagents, and chemicals, you will be able to start.

On hearing this, all the scientists once again applauded enthusiastically since Jill, one of their comrades, suggested a clever idea. Professor Hunter also joined the applause. Without hesitation, Jill and Armand bought copious amounts of the drugs that Jill wanted and many chemicals. Professor Hunter, who held a license as a practicing psychologist, although he did not practice, supplied them with enough prescriptions so that they could start their work at once. He told them also that they have large sums of money at their disposal to buy whatever else they need. He also hired for them, and the rest of the scientists, a purchasing clerk by the name of Anselmo Corton who will buy everything that they will need. Jill and Armand were happy upon hearing this information, since they were afraid that they will have to spend a lot of time purchasing chemicals and reagents. Both started to work to modify one drug at a time and subjected it to all the organic chemistry reactions of their trade: Nucleophilic and electrophilic addition and radical addition, subtraction, oxidation and reduction, rearrangements, elimination, and so on.

The professor finished the meeting after asking if anybody had a question and nobody had. professor Hunter bade all of them success and invited them to a" happy hour" with drinks and with Perl's "goodies" in the conference room.

Even before Professor Hunter chose his team, he already worked hard to prepare for the start of work by buying a lot of modern and expensive equipment. He spent a lot of money on DNA-, RNA- and peptide synthesizers, the most up-to-date automatic DNA and RNA and protein sequencers, and many more instruments. He placed his purchases carefully since all of them were necessary to meet the requirements of his projected ideas of the first and second steps.

The instruments were also going to be "bribe" all the scientists of the department as a "dowry", to satisfy the commitments that he made to the Board of regents, the Dean, and the Chairman of the Department. Professor Hunter also figured that if he failed in Donner's project and even if he succeeded, he would donate all the machines and instruments to the department of psychology. As a result, he received permission from Professor Henriké and the

Dean of the faculty to take over the second spacious lab that belonged to a retired professor and was currently empty.

It should be mentioned, however, that the scientists of the psychology department may not have any use for the equipment since most of their studies were derived from the Humanities' areas. Professor Hunter knew that if his start-up dissolved, or if he completed its mission, the equipment would revert to the Chemistry/protein Chemistry department of Berkley University.

The professor paid for contracts for repairs and maintenance from the instruments' supply companies. Since Professor Hunter poured large bonuses to the instrument-companies for quick delivery of all the instrumentation, they worked amazingly fast and quickly installed everything. They also validated all the instruments after their installation, to ensure that everything is in perfect working order and that the values that they will deliver upon use, will be the correct ones, according to standards.

After the installation of the instruments and the acceptance of the start-up within the psychology department by its chairperson and the dean of the school, Professor Hunter let Yohan Donner know that the first milestone had been reached. Donner sent him back a "well-done" mail.

Then, after his successful recruitment of all the post-docs and residents that he needed, the professor updated Donner again that the second milestone had been reached and listed the names and the scientific specialization of each one of his team. He did it because he knew that Donner had told him that he had some tuition in the life-sciences subjects and could appreciate his choices. Again, Donner sent him a confirmation and a satisfaction mail.

After that the professor's idea on the anti-receptor blockers had been presented to his team and accepted by them, and Jill's pharmacologist idea on the drug-induced Anosmia was starting to run, another milestone crossing report had been sent to Donner. It had been received with the same enthusiasm as before.

Chapter 13:
The resection of the VMO

Every week on Mondays and Fridays, Professor Hunter's team met at 10:00 to report on any developments that they may have made in the preceding week and to have a planning session of actions for future work.

In one of these sessions, Jill was forced to admit that she was stymied. All their attempts to produce a "conversion" by inducing complete anosmia in Bernard and in the other paid gay person subjects failed. They could still smell the synthetic Androsterone and some drug modifications in the molecules of the drugs even completely abolished the partial anosmia of their original composition and caused allowed free smelling.

The project of the organic/Protein chemists to synthesize the eight receptor peptides of the VMO was already completed. The eight synthesized receptors were delivered to the Immunochemists who linked them to BSA and injected each pair of rabbits with a single BSA-Receptor combination. However, it would still be 3 months at least before they will start to bleed the rabbits to harvest the anti-receptor (and the unnecessary anti BSA) antibodies.

In one of the Monday meeting, Professor Hunter started the session and said: "We still need to know if by "knocking off" the VMO receptors, we can, indeed convert homosexuality to heterosexuality. If such a "knocking off" will not work, then our antibody idea will also fail, and we may lose three months of worthless waiting. Unfortunately, the rabbits work at their own pace, although there are impatient scientists who wish to find if paralysis of the eight receptors on the VMO may eliminate gay tendencies, Therefore I have an alternative idea that I am going to present to you now: Note that this idea is illegal! If it becomes known, then as the CEO and the investigator-in-charge of our start-up, I shall lose my psychologist's license, I shall also have to pay heavy damages to the subjects of my projected trial and I may even end up in jail. I intend to use human subjects in a small clinical trial that will cause them some bodily harm! This is contrary to the rules of any clinical trial! Can anybody guess what this trial is going to be?" Dr, June Meers, the Ear, Nose and Throat resident at once burst in: "Nu, Yah, Herr Brovessor! Ve are goink to distroy the VMO itself in our subjects mit einen shkalpel!" Happily, Professor Hunter said: "Yes, June, indeed! I knew that you would know the answer, since ENT surgery is your bread and butter..."

Professor Hunter continued: "To minimize my personal risk, I shall use the help of our evangelist sponsor, Yohan Donner. He is the pastor of a large Evangelical Church that he built for his community with money that he generously donated. He had already admitted to his parish that his son, Axel, is a gay person and that he had hired us to find a way to convert his son to homosexuality and whoever else in the world who might be interested. Because of his work with us, His parish accepted his admission of his son's gay activity without leaving his church.

Following the failure of the drug-anosmia trial, I wrote to Yohan, our sponsor, of my VMO's surgery idea and asked him if there are any gay people among his parish. He answered me that a few persons of his parish had approached him, and "came out of the closet." I asked him further to see if he can find among them some persons who would not mind the possible loss of all sexual desire for men because of the nose operation that they will undergo. He came back and said that three of the gay people are not young anymore. They do not care if their desire for men or women will completely disappear because of the surgery that they will undergo. When Donner questioned them, they said that they will "go happily under the knife" to help his son. Donner even went further, had them sign a notary release freeing us from any responsibility (although this release will not hold up in court). To strengthen their resolve, Donner paid each of them a million dollars to secure their agreement further … He said that he will use his jet to transfer the men to us. The three gay people agreed to wear a blood-pressure monitor around their private members, while they watch pornographic movies of naked young or old, handsome, or ugly men making love, before and after their operation."

"June," said the professor to Dr. Meers "I am sure that you know your way inside noses after having performed surgery on many of them with Dr. Win. Would you do these VMO surgeries for us?"

June answered happily: "Oh, of course I would. I started to fear that you have invited an ENT resident to your team only as an ornament… Truly, I am extremely attractive, but not that much…" All her team-mates burst out laughing since she said that with a complete poker face, while in truth she was very pretty and sexy…

Professor Hunter said: "Good, then that is settled. In addition, take it from an old, experienced man, you are certainly attractive, no sexual harassment meant, but not that much…" the team guffawed again…

The evangelist parishioners from Donner's church arrived quickly from Norman, Oklahoma and were settled in a pleasant hotel in Berkley. Professor Hunter pulled a few strings in the Berkley's University Hospital and managed, with the help of a donation, to rent an ENT operating theater for Dr. Meers.

Dr. Meers dug into the evangelists' noses under a local anesthetic and basing on her experience with Dr. Win, managed to find the vestigial VMO with its receptors and nerves, and resected them out. The evangelist patients required two days to recuperate until the blood flow in the location of the surgery clotted and the wound healed. Dr. Meers praised the three men for their forbearance during and after the surgery. She said that she wished that all her patients in the past had shown such self-restraint… However, it must be honestly said that none of her past patients could console themselves with thoughts of a million dollars present!

Before surgery, the three evangelists were exposed to pornographic movies of gay people in an atmosphere of amounts of artificially synthesized 'Androsterone' pheromone. This was to establish a background of positive gay response of blood pressure in their penises. The blood pressure responses graphs were recorded during the screening of the movies. Then, after the evangelists recuperated from the surgery, they were subjected again to the same conditions as those before the surgery. The "before" and "after" penises' blood pressure graphs were presented to the scientists and clearly proved the fact that the resection of the VMOs plus receptors in the evangelists' noses completely abolished their gay preferences.

Dr. Meers and Professor Hunter were congratulated on their success, which showed that the antibody project now gained a lot of respectability!

Chapter 14:
The Temptation

To become more acquainted with his employees, Professor Hunter decided to dedicate the early Monday mornings to sit with each of the scientists in his office for an in-depth, informal interviews. For each interview, he planned to show each scientist his own family's photographs, to learn more about the personal biographies of his team, and about each one's past achievements in their research. He also wanted to invite them and their boyfriends or wives to a barbecue at his home on the Sunday after the completion of all interviews.

First, He invited Dr. June Meers, the ENT resident who showed in her application mail that she had worked with Dr. Win who discovered in 2015 evidence of residual VMOs in cadavers and live patients. The professor wanted to learn about her experience in Win's lab. He just wanted to become familiar with all his scientists, but he got much more than he bargained for...:

Early on the Monday morning, Dr. Meers came to his office, and Professor Hunter was taken aback when he saw her: She did not wear a bra and her flimsy and transparent shirt barely concealed her beautiful, surgically improved breasts. Her skirt had a long slit going all the way to her groin. She sat in the chair with spread legs which clearly showed an absence of any panties and the presence of a crown of blond pubic hair. The professor was then "attacked" with strong wafts of perfume and pheromone.

He was mesmerized and could not withdraw his eyes from her inviting female equipment. Confused, he mumbled some welcome words and then, panting heavily, he asked her if she will bring her boyfriend to a Sunday barbecue that he plans to hold for all the scientists and their families in his garden.

Dr. Meers answered: "I don't have a boy-friend. All the men in my age bracket that I have dated in the past, were gross and inconsiderate, and just wanted to enter quickly into my panties! I am drawn to older men like you, who know how to entice and foreplay with a girl before the actual act..."

Professor Hunter tried hard to cling to some remnant of respectability. He felt that all his blood is streaming wildly to his face and to his unruly sexual extremity... He turned his gaze to the photograph of his family as if trying to obtain some support from them...

He thought for a few seconds and then, with a contracted and hoarse throat he managed to say: "Dr. Meers, I see that you are blatantly offering yourself to me. However, I am a married man and I love my wife. True, she is a bit older than me, and in the last few years had lost any interest in sex. It is a situation common in many women of her age. As a result, I am lacking in this area of, er... sex. But I cannot accept your offer, although you are so enticing, alluring and sexy... If I will engage in sex with you and it will become known, it will sabotage our common work and I will lose my integrity in the eyes of our team. Also, I do not want to hurt my wife. You cannot realize how sorry I am, but I must ask you now to leave the team!!..."

Dr. Meers approached the professor very closely and brushed her body against him saying: "Professor, you don't know what you are missing! We can have immeasurable pleasure together! However, if you choose to avoid it, can I still stay if I promise to restrain myself? You saw how proficient I am in my medical profession! The surgery that I performed on our three evangelists was a sounding success, was it not?"

Glumly Professor Hunter pushed her gently away from him and said: "No, Dr. Meers, I am sorry! Contrary to my real wish, I will have to notify your colleagues that you received the results of a medical test that you took before you came here, and it caused you to leave at once to start treatment. I shall say good-bye to them in your stead. However, I shall compensate you very handsomely for the loss of your earlier job and because you will have to break the lease on your new home that you just rented in Berkley, although it is not my fault! Leave me your address and I will send you the check forthwith!"

Crestfallen, Dr. Meers left the office, and the professor sat several minutes shaking his head in regret... Later in the day, he called Mary and asked her to search among the old e-mails for the address of another ENT applicant, a Dr. Wolf Schweizer who previously was not chosen, and to invite him to an acceptance interview. He explained to her why: "Dr. Meers had to leave," and Mary shortly commiserated with her and went to do the professor's bidding.

However, a few days later, Professor Hunter was buoyed by the success of his VMO's resection idea, and being carried away on this wave of satisfaction, he began to re-think about his earlier rejection of Dr. Meers. He told himself that life is short, that he is 65 years old and may not live ten years from now, since he came from a short-lived genetic stock. He never "took advantage" of female students or female associates who signaled him that they would like to become "friendly" with him. His only chance of ever enjoying sex now, short of paying for it... is zero! He struggled with the thought for a long time. On one hand he loved his wife and did not want to betray her, insult her, and lose his integrity. In the next minute he thought that she may not be too angry if she will find out about his infidelity, because she knew that she no longer fulfilled her "marital duties". Then he was afraid that his sons may side with his wife if a conflict will erupt.

Finally, the picture of June's sexy naked body lying invitingly, waiting for his caresses, was the last straw. (He now thought of her as "June" instead of "Dr. Meers"). He hoped that she will take him back into her life for one last spree of Spring, despite his earlier rejection...

He picked up the phone several times and then changed his mind back and forth. Finally, he made the call: "Dr. Meers, Hi. It is I, Jack, Jack Hunter. Err. I..." He stuttered.

June at once cut his talk: "Hi, Jack, what took you so long?! I knew that you would change your mind about me... I had not applied for a job elsewhere but waited for your call! Dear Jack, come to me! I want you with all my heart and body…"

Professor Hunter felt as if he is an actor in a grade "B" Bollywood's romantic movie and he scoffed at himself and at the situation into which he was thrown. Still, he was grateful to June for making it so easy and so casually for him to return to her... June told him her address in the apartment that she rented and never relinquished, being sure that her professor will finally seek her out.

He called Mary and told her to re-invite June to work, saying that he received a mail from her that the earlier warning she had received, was a false alarm. He also told Mary to call Dr. Schweizer and apologize to him and explain the situation of the return of an applicant who was previously accepted and her false alarm.

The professor ordered a cab, and before his scruples got the better of him, he went to his 'love nest." It must be said, though, that obviously, it was not love that caused him to reach June's apartment, but pure lust, satisfying sex, between two consenting adults... As a scientist who dealt all his life with various forms of lust, he finally caved in, hoping desperately that his wife will not learn about his infidelity.

Since he started with the project he used to come home late at night because of his employment as the CEO and chief scientist of the start-up. As a result, he felt confident that he will be able to hide his infidelity.

June welcomed him at the door dressed very scantily and when she saw that her boss-lover was shaking like a leaf in a wind because of being new to the experience, she immediately embraced him and sealed his lips with a fervent kiss before he could make a spectacle of himself... Apparently, she was experienced in the seduction of celibate older husbands that had been faithful to their wives for too long...

I do not intend to satisfy the voyeurism of my readers with long pornographic descriptions of the first encounter, and those that followed it. Suffice it to say, that the first sex encounter between them was a flop. As expected, it ended in a minute... Professor Hunter did not even have time to apologize. June held him to her breast, kissed him hotly on his lips and elsewhere, until he recuperated... the second and third encounter between them in that long evening was longer and left both fulfilled and glowing. It left the professor happy and clear-headed, strengthened his scientific acumen and weakened his sense of guilt. Finally, Professor Hunter took a long shower and then asked June to refrain from the use of perfume before their pre-arranged meetings lest his betrayal will be known to his wife Flora or to his more acute smelling colleagues. June, experienced in these matters, and not willing to lose her job and her new lover, of course agreed.

The professor made June promise him that she will always dress modestly to work and never show him any affection in public. June promised to behave and to be careful with her behavior.

Chapter 15:
Re-appraisal of phase two of the research

Early one morning, relaxed after a happy encounter in the night before with June, Professor Hunter started to think on a solution to phase two of the projects. This phase was intended to cause Axel to become susceptible to women's sexual allure (and pheromones). Also, to have him marry, make love to his bride and present Donner with a grandson or a granddaughter, or both.

Professor Hunter envisioned June lying satisfied and naked on her bed as he last saw her when he left her apartment last night... From this happy thought, he went on, to try to guess whether the rabbits are doing their share of work in the production of the antibodies against the VMO's pheromone receptors. Yet, it was early, and the rabbits were not even sample-bled for the ELISA assay. Then he suddenly froze in his tracks!

In his past scientific studies, he had studied the thought-provoking situation that was allowing gay people to support their percentage in the population and even increase in number. Since they do not want to copulate with women, the number of gay people in the world should have gradually decreased, up to their disappearance. The answers that came to him and to other population experts were several and were already discussed above.

The reason that Professor Hunter froze in his tracks was because he realized that Yohan Donner and his son Axel, will be vexed when they will find about the sexual orientation of the Donner heir

(Axel's son). His sexual orientation will be entirely gay! You may ask why? Well, here is why:

As a result of the anti-receptor treatment, (or even of an ENT surgery, if the antibodies will not work), Axel will be without his male preference. But he will not be attracted to women and will NOT be able to copulate with his bride and give Donner a much-coveted heir. It is true that Axel will be "non-gay" on the outside, that is phenotypically, because of the anti-receptor treatment. But genetically, all his cells will still carry X chromatids containing the crossed-over homosexuality gene(s)! Therefore, he may force himself to fertilize a wife, but will still transfer homosexual genetic information **to his offspring**. Professor Hunter realized that Donner's grandson will be born, most certainly, a gay person. He will still find it necessary (if he will also be evangelical), to undergo the same antibody treatment or an ENT resection as his father did, and so will his progeny after him forever!...

The outshot of the treatments meant that he will not be able to fulfil his promise to Donner just by the antibody or ENT resection methods. He realized that his work was still cut out for him: He will still have to find a way intervene genetically in the Donner embryo to make him and his progeny forever real heterosexuals.

While waiting for the rabbits to reach the highest antibody titer, Professor Hunter asked the scientists who were not employed in the sampling and testing of the antibodies to turn to an important scientific job. They were asked to determine the nucleotide sequence of the homosexuality genes – polymorphisms - in the Xq28 region of the X chromosome and in the peri-centromeric region of chromosome 8. This was going to be done by searching for polymorphisms (mutations) in the DNAs of several gay people in comparison the DNA sequences of straight people!

Most obviously, this was because the professor wanted to be prepared for a genetic repair of the Donner baby. To his scientists he explained the rationale for the new project by saying that company has many up-to-date instruments. Therefore, he explained, he wants to make use of the instruments, He said that if they succeeded in determining the sequence of homosexuality genes and will publish it, it might make an important "splash" scientifically. Once published it will help all post-docs to obtain good tenured academic jobs when they leave. The postdocs did not require much impetus after they heard this and started to work diligently thereby fending for themselves and laying, unbeknown to them, the ground for a genetic intervention in the Donner baby's DNA.

It then occurred to the professor that subconsciously he was prepared for such an eventuality when he hired not one, but two molecular geneticists. This made him realize how powerful the intuition of a good scientist can be. He himself did not know yet what kind of intervention it would be. He will have to ask his molecular geneticists when the time comes. However, he realized that the baby would have to be conceived in an IVF process with Axel's sperm and his future wife's ovum. This is the only way the Donner heir and his next offspring will become straight by a genetic intervention!

Professor Hunter decided not to broach the subject of a genetic intervention to Donner and his to postdocs just yet. He decided that the time for that will come after a success of the antibodies' project.

Chapter 16:
The blocking of the VMO's receptors with antibodies

The rabbits in the animal house of Berkley, courtesy of a handsome donation to the department of life sciences, thrived, grew in weight, and caused Hunter's immuno-chemists to develop "vampire" (bleeding…) appetites. However, before these appetites could be satisfied, the immuno-chemists needed to learn when the rabbits will be "ripe" for harvest.

Those animal rights activists among our readers should not worry. Each bi-weekly trial bleeding from the ear vein was stopped after the bleeding of about 20 milliliters of blood, which after clotting gave 10 ml of serum. This action did not harm the rabbits even a little bit. The trial bleedings were performed by warming the rabbit's ear under a regular reading lamp and nicking one of the heat-extended ear veins with a scalpel. The nick yielded a slow flow of blood into a tube. The flow of blood was stemmed after the necessary amount blood was obtained. The bleeding for the final harvests was similar, except that the blood flow was stopped after 50 milliliters. Even here the rabbits recovered quickly after all the bleedings. The testing of the 10 ml trial bleedings started in the ELISA plates at 2 months after the start of the immunizations (which included also 4 more weekly injections of BSA-receptor combinations in the first 4 weeks). Since each of the eight receptor-BSA combinations was injected into two rabbits, this resulted in

16 samples for the ELISA test every two weeks. The sixteen bi-weekly serum samples that were tested, showed uniform results which are presented in the table below.

Results of the titration of the rabbit trial antisera by ELISA

Receptor name and class	Bleeding times of the Rabbits (weeks since start of the immunization) showing the last positive dilution in the ELISA plates (antibody titer)							
	8	10	12	14	16	20	22	24
V1R short*)	1:8	1:16	1:32	1:128	1:256	1:256	1:256	1:256
V1R short*)	1:4	1:16	1:32	1:64	1:128	1:256	1:256	1:256
TAR short*)	1:4	1:16	1:32	1:64	1:128	1:256	1:256	1:256
TAR short*)	1:4	1:16	1:32	1:64	1:128	1:256	1:256	1:256
TAAR5 short*)	1:8	1:16	1:32	1:128	1:256	1:256	1:256	1:256
TAAR5 short*)	1:8	1:16	1:32	1:128	1:256	1:256	1:256	1:256
V2R long**)	1:16	1:64	1:64	1:128	1:256	1:512	1:512	1:512
V2R long**)	1:8	1:16	1:64	1:128	1:256	1:512	1:512	1:512
TAAR6 long**)	1:16	1:64	1:64	1:128	1:256	1:512	1:512	1:512
TAAR6 long**)	1:16	1:64	1:64	1:128	1:256	1:512	1:512	1:512
TAAR8 long**)	1:8	1:32	1:128	1:128	1:256	1:512	1:512	1:512
TAAR8 long**)	1:64	1:64	1:128	1:128	1:256	1:512	1:512	1:512
TAAR9 long**)	1:16	1:64	1:64	1:128	1:256	1:512	1:512	1:512
TAAR9 long**)	1:16	1:64	1:64	1:128	1:256	1:512	1:512	1:512
FPR long**)	1:16	1:64	1:64	1:128	1:256	1:512	1:512	1:512
FPR long**)	1:16	1:64	1:64	1:128	1:256	1:512	1:512	1:512

*) Short receptor that connect to sensory neurons synapsing to the posterior part of the Accessory olfactory bulbs.

**) Long receptor that connect to neurons deep in the anterior part of the accessory olfactory bulbs.

As can be seen in the table, the long receptors gave slightly higher anti-repressor antibodies than those of the short repressors. Each row of the ELISA plates had the tested repressor attached to the Elisa plate so that only the anti-repressor antibodies were assayed and not the anti-BSA antibodies.

The results of the 20, 22 and 24 weeks after start of the immunization showed that the rabbits had reached their peak production of antibodies at that date; In view of the results, the eager "vampire" scientists bled about 50 milliliters of blood every 4 days starting from the 25th week up to the 28th week, then they separated the serum and pooled it. Next, the antisera against the individual repressors from each pair of rabbits were passed through the anti-BSA columns and the happy scientists recovered pure anti repressor antibodies for the blocking experiments of the homosexuality preference in the evangelistic paid "volunteers" and in Armand.

The scientists applied the anti-receptor antibodies singly, but both the evangelical volunteers and Armand continued to "enjoy" the pornographic movies with a complete disregard of the inhibitors of gay preference that were applied to their noses.

The disappointed scientists, who were hoping for an inhibitory response with a single antibody against a single receptor in order induce a heterosexuality preference in Axel, failed. Even when they applied pooled three antisera against the short receptors alone or the pooled 5 antisera against five long receptors, they could not block the receptors. Only when they pooled all the different antisera together, they were able to obtain a complete abolishment of the gay preference.

Professor Hunter called the scientists to a summary meeting on the antibodies' trial . They came to the meeting with high spirits hoping that the professor will tell them to get out the Champagne bottles that were cooling in the refrigerators in the kitchen. But this was not to be.

Instead, of raising a toast, the professor, with a serious mien, started to speak: "Dear colleagues, A few days ago Armand pointed to me that he thinks the weekly instillation of the pool of antibodies will be a serious burden. Moreover, Among the eight antibodies of the total pool, there are antibodies with various affinities to the receptors and those with the low affinity will slough early off from their receptors. and ooze out from the nose. Therefore, our plan to block homosexuality will be viable for only a **short** week, because we need all the antibodies to act in tandem to block the receptors.

As a result, Armand, who brought the "short week" phenomenon to my attention, suggested an excellent idea. I shall let Armand describe It. OK, Armand, speak up and may your words shine..."

Armand stood up and said: "Thank you, boss. Fellows, I want to suggest that we will link the antibodies to the receptors permanently.

Most protein–protein linking attempts fail, Binding of one protein type to another through biding are transient and occur only briefly with the purpose to help a quick signaling or metabolic function. But, to obtain a constant capturing or freezing of these momentary contacts, cross-linking reagents must be added. These cross-linking reagents capture and stabilize the protein-protein complexes (antibody-receptor in our case). Strong, and permanent linking of proteins is then achieved by the covalently binding of the linkers between the edges of the 2 target proteins. There are two types of linkers: flexible linkers and rigid linkers. Some of the linkers are quite long and complicated. Many types of linkers consist of short or long peptides based on repeats of glycine-serine-alanine. One of the most popular linkers is made of repeats of the sequence: (Gly-Gly-Gly-Gly-Ser, multiplies several times). The best length is decided by trial and error. We shall try to use the smallest number of repeats of (Gly-Gly-Gly-Gly-Ser) to link the rabbit antibody on one side, and the short and long receptor peptides that are attached to the VMO on the other side.

I suggest that I and Jerry will synthesize just one linker length at a time. Then we shall apply each synthesized linker to the nose of our volunteers after they had been treated with the mix of antibodies. Next, we shall apply a weak acidic nose drops to shear off the rabbit antibodies. If the linker did not attach, the antibodies will leave the receptors. Then we shall test the evangelists with the pornographic movies. If the tested linker will bind between the receptors and the rabbit antibodies, the receptors will be paralyzed. And the evangelists will not react to the movies.

Armand completed his suggestion and both professor hunter and the scientists reacted with enthusiastic applause.

The professor asked the evangelistic "guineas pigs" to stay for the linker experiments a few more weeks in Berkley to ensure that the linker mechanism will be sequentially tested. The evangelists were happy to stay some more, to enjoy the hotel's luxuries and the viewing of pornographic movies as before. And all that for the easy work of the instillation of some fluids into their noses…

Armand and Jerry started to produce linkers with the help of the protein/peptide synthesizing machine. The sequence of the linkers that each one of them was synthesized was verified by a protein sequencer machine to see if the protein synthesizer was exact in its syntheses. Then the synthesized linkers were, of course, applied to the evangelists' noses after they were first treated with antibodies.

Josh and Jerry found out that, luckily, all the simple linker peptides of the formulas (Gly-Gly-Gly-Gly-Gly-Ser) repeated 5 to 11 times, worked well. They inked the receptor and antibody mix tightly.

As the story of the antibodies plus linkers plus sloughing-off of the receptor proved to be feasible, the scientists rejoiced, even though it was at the expense of the blocking of all the VMO receptors.

Professor Hunter let Donner know of the success of the Rabbit antibody project plus the linker story and the sloughing off of the receptor. But, at the same information-reporting phone call, the professor also admitted that in phase 2 of their trial – the attempt to convert Axel genetically and permanently to heterosexuality had not made any break-through whatsoever. Donner consoled hunter and said that Rome was not built in one day and that he is completely confident that Hunter with his scientists will eventually succeed in solving the problem…

Chapter 17:
The Genetic Correction of the Donner Fetus

Meanwhile, simultaneously with the scientists who were busy with the rabbit antibodies, their application to the gay test candidates and the linking of the antibodies, the molecular geneticists were also busy: They determined the sequence of the homosexuality fragments of DNA- in the Xq28 region of the X chromosome and in the peri-centromeric region of chromosome 8 . But they were especially happy since they discovered 3 additional polymorphisms in 3 previously unknown chromosomes.

Jim, Armand, Jerry, and Josh achieved these important discoveries by comparing the DNA sequences of the 5 volunteer evangelists and of Armand to their own DNAs. The comparisons used WGS (Whole Genome Sequencing) that was carried out with automatic DNA sequencers.

The scientists used the two modern DNA sequencers in the department's equipment room that Professor Hunter bought even before he knew if any scientist from his team will use them. Professor Hunter was happy with this result and divulged his secret to the team, that he wants the company's molecular geneticists Armand, and Jim, to use the data in the conversion of the Donner fetus. Also, he said that they can publish a paper that will reveal to the world the additional polymorphisms that are responsible for homosexuality that they discovered. He said that he will write the first draft and all the post-docs will be co-authors by alphabetical order and will help to edit the paper. He also added that he will send the manuscript to "Nature reviews genetics" and that he is sure that it will be accepted because of its merit, and besides, he added: "I am friendly with all scientists in the editorial board..."

The scientists were happy with Professor Hunter's decision, But Jim said: "Professor, by rights, the principal investigator, namely you, should be the first author on the paper. Why are you disregarding this privilege?" The boss answered: "Jim, my friend, I have a lot of papers in my CV, and I am a full professor who is about to retire, once we achieve our goal. Therefore, I do not need this priority. The first author on our paper will be chosen by lottery" Jim accepted the explanation and his disgruntlement subsided. Then the professor added: "Some time ago, a Finnish investigator by the name of Ganna and his collaborators, also used WGS like us to find polymorphisms. Their study revealed five SNPs - Single nucleotide polymorphisms - that were significantly associated with same-sex preference. Two of the five polymorphisms were detected in both men and women, two others in men alone and one in women only. In aggregate, all the discovered genetic polymorphisms accounted for 8 to 25% of gay or lesbian behavior. The study was revealing, but it should be noted that SNPs do not conform to our polymorphisms, which cover and identify large genome fragments. "

The scientists barely had time to digest the professor Hunter's words when he continued: "We have the right to rejoice on the future publication of our paper. However, I want to tell you that a few days ago I came to the stunning and unhappy conclusion that we are still far from Donner's target. Just treating Axel with antibodies and to fix them in place with linkers is just a small step forward!

True, we shall cure him of his gay tendency with the rabbit antibodies plus linker. However, while at face value he is indeed a 'non-gay". He is Genetically still a gay person! All his cells, including his sperm cells, still be stamped genetically with the gay genes. Not only that, but any son that he might have, will be gay too. We have not completed a key factor of mandate! We shall have to intervene genetically in Axel's fetus before he is born and matures sexually!

You may ask what kind a of genetic intervention we shall have to use? I must admit that, at present, I so not have any idea. We shall have to consult our molecular geneticists. Up to now they worked diligently on the unravelling of the sequences of the homosexuality inducing genes.

I am sure, though, that we shall have to use this sequencing information that Armand and Jim discovered. I do hope that Armand and Jim will also be able instruct us on how to correct the homosexuality inclination that Axel's son will inherit from his father! Armand and Jim, can you do it? I shall give you one week to find us some idea how to do it"

Jim answered: "Boss I never saw any conversion ideas in the molecular genetic literature." And Armand said: "Boss, I do hope that Jim and I shall be able to come back to you with some ideas. I must say, though, that I too never saw in the genetic literature any solution for the problem that you posed to us."

The Professor then said: "well then, in this case we shall have to invent our own solutions!!!" With this statement Professor Hunter closed the meeting... As a result of the meeting both Armand and Jim started to spend long hours in the Psychology and the Genetics library of Berkley.

A week later, all the scientists convened again for another meeting, to hear whether Armand and Jim could suggest a good plan to convert the Donner heir to <u>genetic</u> heterosexual preference.

Armand spoke first and said "Dear colleagues. Jim and I reached a unanimous decision on how to solve the conversion of the Donner fetus. We decided that Jim, who is the more erudite among us, will describe it."

Jim stood up and started to speak: "Boys and girls, and Boss, here is our proposal: The first part of the proposal will be to outsource since we do not have the right facility and the experience to do it: When the time comes for Axel to find a sweetheart to marry (in his non-gay state), we shall ask the couple to undergo an IVF procedure (In Vitro Fertilitzation) in a maternity ward and a genetic hospital that they shall choose. Once they will finish the process, it will be our turn to act. For those who are not familiar with the steps of the IVF process, I prepared slides that I will soon screen to you.

After the screening, Armand shall describe to you the idea that we concocted.

Jim screened slides one after the other in a speed that would allow reading:

DESCRIPTION OF THE IVF PROCESS

Step 1: The stimulation phase

The first official day of the IVF treatment cycle is day 1 of the woman's period. The stimulation phase starts then.

In an unstimulated natural monthly cycle, the woman's ovaries normally produce just one egg (ovum). In an IVF, the woman takes a medication for 8-14 days to encourage the ovarian follicles to produce more ova.

The application of the stimulating medication is usually in the form of hormone injections, which can vary from 1-2 injections for the whole cycle, or 1-2 injections per day.

The most common hormones are follicle-stimulating hormone (FSH), and luteinizing hormone (LH).

Both hormones are produced naturally in the body. The eggs are already there; but the medication boosts the natural levels of the hormones to encourage more eggs to develop.

Step 2: The trigger phase

The ovaries are watched with blood tests and ultrasounds to see how the follicles are developing. The concentration of the medication is adjusted if needed. The woman is tracked more often towards the end of the stimulation phase to time the 'trigger injection' perfectly.

The trigger injection gets the eggs ready for ovulation. In the natural process it is when the egg (ovum) is released, and the woman gets her period. In the IVF process, the fertility specialist will schedule the egg retrieval <u>before</u> the woman ovulates.

Step 3: Egg retrieval

The eggs are collected from the ovaries under a general anesthetic. The retrieval takes about 20-30 minutes. Ultrasound is used to guide a needle into the "ripe" follicles in each of the two ovaries. The eggs are contained in fluid within the follicles. The fluid is removed from those follicles which look like they have grown enough to have an egg inside. The average number of eggs harvested in each IVF process is 8-15.

Step 4: The sperm

In the morning of the ova's retrieval, the male (Axel) produces a sample of sperm. The sample is washed in a special mixture to slow the swimming sperm cells down, so that the doctors can spot the best ones under the microscope. A perfect, healthy sperm is not too fat nor too thin and with a tail that is not too long or too short. The best-looking sperm cells are selected, and they wait in anticipation for the happy encounter with the ova.

It is important to fertilize the ova quickly. The ova and some sperm are placed in a dish. They have the chance to find each other and fertilize as they would naturally within the woman's body.

Step 5: Embryo development

If the sperm fertilizes the eggs, they become embryos. The embryos are put in an incubator in a mix of amino acids, The embryos are watched over 5-6 days. On day 2 the embryos have two- to four-cells and on day 3 they have a six-to eight-cell (called the cleavage stage). On day 3 they already are in what is called the blastocyst stage.

Stage 6: Embryo transfer

An embryo transfer to the uterus is an uncomplicated process. It takes about 5 minutes. The embryo is placed in catheter that goes through into the uterus. One embryo that underwent a successful conversion to heterosexuality by us, as I will soon describe, will be placed in the uterus and the rest of the embryos are frozen for use in additional genetic conversion treatment in case we fail with our first trial.

Step 7: The final blood test

Two weeks after the embryo transfer, the woman will have a blood test to measure the level of her hCG hormone (human chorionic gonadotropin). hCG in the bloodstream usually means a positive pregnancy.

Now I shall transfer the baton to Armand who will continue with our proposal." Armand started: "In the past, there existed a method to correct a faulty gene in the fetus that was to act on the growing fetus in the woman's womb when they are five to six months old, weigh two pounds, and measure a foot. At this stage, a DNA fragment with the healthy genetic material is delivered with a long needle that pierces the mother's uterus, penetrating the umbilical cord, together with a gene-editing-tool which is the CrisperCas9.

Another way to insert the healthy genetic material, is with the use of a benign virus that had been changed so that it cannot replicate. It is loaded with the healthy genes, using again a gene-editing tool like CrisperCas9. This benign virus would infect the defective cells of the fetus and replace a missing or defective gene with a good gene, but since the virus cannot multiply in the cells, it does not harm the mother, The CRISPR technology is a simple yet powerful tool for editing genomes. It allows researchers to alter DNA sequences and change gene functions easily.

"CRISPR" stands for "clusters of regularly interspaced short palindromic repeats." It is a specialized piece of DNA with two distinct factors: nucleotide repeats and spacers. Repeated sequences of nucleotides are the building blocks of corrective DNA that are distributed throughout the CRISPR region. Spacers are bits of DNA that are interspersed among these repeated sequences.

I shall not describe this fetus transfer method further since it will not be used by us. The problem with this method is that in case of a genetic failure, the woman (Axel's projected wife) will have to undergo one or more abortions of 5-months old embryos!

Instead, we shall work on 5-day Fetuses using an improved DNA technic developed recently by scientists from Cambridge University: they developed a technology that allows to cut and transfer long stretches of DNA from one genome to another. The CRISPR was changed so that it cuts long pieces of DNA. It uses an enzyme called "lambda red Recombinase" that cuts DNA and circularizes it to protect it from the damaging cell enzymes. The faulty DNA that it cuts can be large - even complete chromosomes can replace out old chromosomes with defects.

Once the Cambridge treatment was performed, we shall have to do a PGS (Pre-implantation Genetic Screening) on a good-looking fertilized blastula with many cells All the rest of the embryos frozen. a single cell or a small number of cells is now removed from the chosen embryo and tested by WGS (whole genetic sequencing of the whole DNA). To get enough DNA for sequencing – that is to determine if they have the corrected gene, the fetal DNA from one cell is multiplied by PCR (Polymerase chain reaction) and only then tested.

Only A tested 5-day old blastula cells whose DNA was found to be free of the homosexuality genes, will be implanted into Axel's putative future wife."

Jim finished his presentation and again he and Armand received their accolade (applause) from their colleagues.

Professor Hunter then said: "We shall have to let Donner know about our fetal correction procedure that Jim and Armand just delineated to us. He might nudge Axel to supply him with a grandchild or a granddaughter right now. But my guess is that he will let Axel finish his studies before he will "saddle" him with a wife and a baby, especially since we did not supply Axel yet with a method which will convert HIM to heterosexuality. Between you and me, I think that this is a task that we can never solve...

The professor called Donner on the phone and told him of the possibility of a grandchild from Axel by IVF and Axel's sperm. Donner was elated, but as expected beforehand by the professor, Axel decided to wait.

Chapter 18:
The use of carbon nanotubes

With the successful solution of the gay preference of the evangelists and Armand, all the scientists and professor Hunter tried hard to find a solution to Donner's request to convert Axel to heterosexuality, and not just his future fetus, and not just to block his gay inclination. Finally, Jim got an idea that was so simple that he himself could not believe that he got it.

To check whether he is not deluding himself, he decided to present his idea to the other Molecular biologist in his team, Armand Ban. He needed his confirmation anyway if he planned to present it to the team. Consequently, he waited for an opportunity to catch Armand alone. This happened a few days later in the evening when both stayed late and alone in the wide lab.

Jim said: "Hey Bernie, listen please, I need your help. I want to present to you an idea that had incubated in me for a whole week. I need you to confirm it, or to tell me to erase it completely, and to send it to the land of unfulfilled and half-baked ideas."

Armand saw that Jim was excited and moved his chair to Jim's desk and said: "OK Brother, I am all ears."

Jim started to narrate his idea as if he is already presenting it y to whole team of post-docs and his boss:

"Here is the proposal that I want to present to you and to the team. It is revolutionary and hypothetical. It deals with the last stage that we still need to solve. The project to convert Axel to heterosexuality.

Professor Hunter taught us that a pheromone's odor sets off an electrical signal in the receptors in and on the Vomeronasal organ. This electrical signal travels from the receptors to an olfactory nerve group in the Vomeronasal Organ. From there it travels to the Limbic system and stimulates a strong lust for men in gay persons.

We know that all of Axel's cells have homosexuality polymorphisms in his DNA. Suppose we change the DNA in the limbic system to 'normalcy" – that is to the un-mutated state? Then the DNA will transcribe RNA that will produce proteins that will recognize pheromone-induced electrical signals that enter the limbic system <u>as coming from copulins and the vaginal aliphatic acids of women!</u>

Currently, we are planning to paralyze Axel's receptors and to remove his homosexuality preference. Conversely, I, on the other hand, suggest that we will not harm them and let them transfer the odor cues and the electrical signals that they will! However, I suggest to cheat the whole of Axel's limbic system to recognize these electrical cues as coming only from sexy women!

Armand listened to Jim's suggestion and said: "Jim, it is a beautiful suggestion, but I see only one fault in it – how are we going to perform this miracle - to fool the limbic system into recognizing gay electric cues as "normal" female ones – that is change, to Axel's DNA in the limbic system and in the Vomeronasal to heterosexual DNA?

Jim continued: "We shall use Carbon nanotubes!!! Tell me, are you acquainted with these materials? No? OK. Then let me describe them:

"Carbon nanotubes are microscopic organic carbon molecules with tubular nanostructures that range between 1 nanometer and 100 nanometers in length and have a nanometer-sized cavity. They are either one-layer-walled, or poly - layer walled.": You know of course, if you have already forgotten, that one nanometer is a billionth of a meter and one millionth of a millimeter. This is how single-walled nanotubes look":

Here Jim opened a reprint of a paper and showed Armand an electron micrograph visage of a single-walled Carbon nanotube:

Carbon Nanotube   **Figure from Hue He et al., Hindawi Biomed Research.**

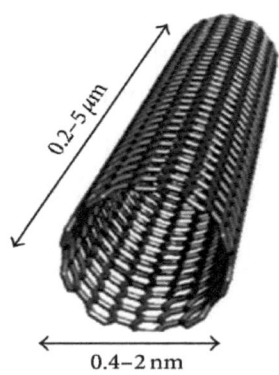

Jim let Armand enough time to be impressed with the photograph, and then continued: "An extremely important application of the Carbon nanotubes is their ability to strongly absorb myriads of complex materials based on carbon, including DNA and many biological materials. Carbon nanotubes loaded with normal fragments of DNA with CRISPRCAS 9 can be internalized by cell! First by binding their tips to cell membrane receptors, then by passing through the cytoplasmic membrane. Once they get into the cell's cytoplasm, they pass through the nuclear membrane into the nucleus with its gay DNA. The CRISP then will correct the DNA to a normal DNA!! Antibiotic drugs or toxic anti-cancer drug inside Carbon nanotubes, had proved to be safer and can safely introduce into cells larger amounts of drugs.

We shall instill the heterosexual normal DNA and CRISPR into Carbon nanotubes. We shall inject the loaded carbon nanotubes straight into the Vomeronasal organ. This way, the heterosexual DNA in the limbic system will produce by transcription and translation proteins that can be only excited by heterosexual signals emitted by women's pheromones. This will be because the heterosexual DNA will produce only "good, "normal-reacting proteins which science does not know yet what they are."

Armand looked surprised and with new eyes at his colleague, and said: "Wow Jim, Hurray! I think you have got it! By George, I think you have got it! It is certainly worth a try! I already see in my mind's eye the important paper that you will publish! I hope that Professor Hunter will put all our names on the paper with you as the senior author! not only that, but our work here will also be finished and on the strength of the paper we can start great academic careers! Moreover, I think that a satisfied Donner will give us remarkably high bonuses!"

But Jim quickly said: "hey Armand, whoa! hold your horses. Money and success are still far away. Do not jinx it! My plan is just a hypothesis now and may fail in practice when we try it". But he was clearly happy and encouraged by Armand's enthusiastic reception."

Then Armand said: "Tell me now how we can produce these "lovely" nanotubes?" Jim answered happily: "There are many technics to produce Carbon nanotubes and many of them use Electrical arc. The simplest way to produce them is from graphite powder at room temperature – a technic that was developed by D. W. Lee, and J. W. Seo: Graphite powder is immersed in a mixed solution of nitric and sulfuric acid with potassium chlorate. After heating the solution up to 70°C and leaving it in air for 3 days, bundles of carbon nanotubes are obtained. This process offers an easy and inexpensive method for the nanotubes' preparation. However, Carbon nanotubes are produced commercially as a powder and are sold very cheaply!"

Jim talked with Armand on Sunday, and he planned to spring his plan in the Monday forum, with Armand "seconding" the motion, and so it was! On Monday, at the start of the weekly brainstorming meeting, Jim said that he has an important suggestion for converting Axel to heterosexuality. The whole team at once perked up their ears because suggestions to convert Axel were rare in the meetings and all of them were, unfortunately, shot down...

Jim started to speak: "Hi friends! I described my idea to Armand, and he was very enthusiastic about it and said that he wants to second the idea! It deals with single walled Carbon nanotubes! Had anybody heard of this material?

Nobody in the meeting has heard about it and Jim instantly went into the description of his idea which was easier to describe a second time (after his exposition to Armand). All the scientists including Professor Hunter sat spellbound through the whole account. When Jim finished, a pandemonium erupted with hand clapping and cries of encouragement!

Professor Hunter asked Jim what it will take to prepare the nanotubes, preferably yesterday. Jim answered: "There are myriad of complicated methods to prepare the Single Walled Carbon Nanotubes (SWCN). But we do not have to use them! Pure powder of SWCN can be bought in kilogram quantities and very cheaply!" Jim showed a photograph of carbon nanotubes' jar from the reprint of the paper that gave him the start of the idea that he presented to the team.

Jim continued: "The powder can be suspended in various aqueous solutions together with our heterosexual synthesized gene fragments and with the improved Cambridge CRISPR that we shall obtain pro gratis from the Cambridge team. The loading of the Carbon nanotubes with our ingredients is quick, but we will leave the suspension for about 24 hours to obtain complete loading. Then our ENT specialist, June, will not have to wait several more months to show her specialty again... She will inject the mixture straight into the VMOs of gay subjects in comparison to a control of "empty" single-walled carbon nanotubes suspension!"

All the participants of Professor Hunter's well- knit team, Including the professor himself, erupted into 10 minutes of wild applause!

Professor Hunter told Jim to ask their purchasing clerk to buy at once several kilograms of pure Carbon nanotubes and said that he will ask Donner to send him by his private jet several new known gay person recruits who will want to convert and to receive million dollars.

Donner was informed of Jim's idea, sent his regards and prayers that the idea will pan out. He hired a "private eye" to find suitable candidates, paid them well to "keep them mum" and sent them in his jet to be tested by Jim and his colleagues

Chapter 19:
"Let my people go (be)!"

The company's purchasing clerk managed to supply Jim and Armand very quickly with one kilogram of Carbon nanotube powder packed in small jars. Armand said that just by looking at the insignificant appearance of the powder, that looked like soot, no one could not imagine the marvelous properties of this material...

After consulting with Armand, Jim concocted the anti-homosexuality-suspension from 3 ingredients: Carbon nanotubes' powder, replicated fragments of heterosexual DNA and the Cambridge CRISPR. The replicated fragments of heterosexual DNA were synthesized in a DNA synthesizer and then multiplied by a PCR process with starters and enders, but without the fluorescent stain. The 3 ingredients were suspended in a physiological salt solution like the one given to patients suffering from extreme sunburn and dehydration in a hospital.

The two scientists also prepared a control suspension that consisted only of Carbon nanotubes suspended in physiological salt solution. Then Jim and Armand left the 2 suspensions for 24 hours at room temperature to complete the loading of the nanotubes.

Night came, and Jim, who was exhausted from the eventful day left home. Armand stayed some more time claiming that he wanted to tidy up the scientists' benches. He was alone in the wide lab except for the cleaner…

Then, Armand, with a heavy heart, poured the DNA-crisper-Carbon nanotubes-loaded suspension into the sink, and washed the empty bottle. Then he added just Carbon nanotube's powder into the bottle with the physiological saline suspension.

He did that because he was sure that, the "**Scuole procedure**," as Jim's technic will be called, will be **used forcibly in the future** on his "brothers," who will be considered a threat due to their multiplication. He believed that this is surely bound to happen as soon as the number of gay persons in the USA and the world would grow, as it is bound to do. Under a Trump-like president, who will be certainly elected, given the increase in the number of roughnecks and ignorant population in the USA, gay people will become an endangered species and will be forced to undergo the Scuole process! He was certain that his act of his counterfeit will not be detected, because none of the suspensions had any telltale differentiating features other than the three typed stickers on the sides of the two bottles!!!

During all the time that he performed his sabotage act, one thought passed his brain: "LET MY PEPLE BE!!! LET MY PEOPLE BE! LET MY PEOPLE GO!" He wanted to free his gay brothers in the future from coercion by governments everywhere!!!

The next day, early in the morning, 6 gay people, wearing blood-pressure measuring instruments on their penises underwent a screening of pornographic gay movies to set up a reference line in the printing gauge. The gay people enjoyed the movies and reacted as expected. Following the screening, and one by one, the 6 gay people, three from each group, were injected expertly into the VMO by June.

The subjects were sent after the injections to their hotel to rest and eat with an invitation to come next day for the pornography tests.

I shall let my intelligent readers decide for themselves what the results were. They did not even change during the next two weeks until the termination of the test...

Chapter 20:
The dissolution of the start-up company

The scientists met for the last Monday morning meeting. The professor praised the role of each of the scientists in the start-up and said that the work with them in the final years of his career, was very uplifting and something that he never expected to happen. Then he said: "I think that we did our best and this is what counts, even though a conversion of Axel did not happen."

Axel and Donner came especially to the start-up for the antibody plus linker treatment, which worked well. The Molecular genetics scientists promised to come from their universities to treat Axel's fetus, once he could find a lovely lady to marry him and to beget children with him.

In the wrap-up meeting Professor hunter said that he spoke with Donner and that the oil magnate is satisfied, mostly because he did not really expect their efforts to succeed all the way. He was happy with the fact that Axel will soon stop being a gay person and that he may have one day a grandson even though he will be genetically gay and only a heterosexual by the antibody-linker treatment.

The professor said that Donner assigned to each of them a "measly" severance-pay of 7 million dollars. The scientists did not believe the professor at first since, after all, their success was limited. But then, they were profuse on the phone with thanks to Donner.

A lot of money remained in start-up's Bank deposit after all the deduction of the expenses. The happy Donner transferred all the remaining money to Professor Hunter's account, and it must be said that this was not a measly sum.

The professor thanked Donner and told him that when he started his scientific career, he never thought, even in his wildest dreams ,that it will become a millionaire. The most that he ever hoped was to earn a Nobel prize with its puny million and some dollars… Donner was happy at Hunter's reaction and both men swore everlasting friendship…

Two special deep freezers were assigned for the reagents that Jim and Armand and June would need in the future for the Donner fetus. The freezers were stored in the Psychology department and were cared for by a reliable, well-compensated employee of the department.

The final meeting of the scientists with their boss was very emotional. The post-docs were happy about the sudden riches that they received, and sad that they will have to depart from dear friends and colleagues and from their boss and mentor who is going to start a "career" of fishing and golf…

The saddest of all the post-docs in the final meeting was Armand who shed large tears, uncommon in a grown-up man and we certainly know why…

The professor and June at last said goodbye. They understood that the enjoyable interlude in their lives ended because the professor will not have an excuse to stay away from home nights. Besides, June wanted to continue her scientific career and was looking forward to new adventures with additional "mature men."

Several years later, Flora admitted to Hunter that she knew that he had an extramarital affair during his work with the start-up, but she did not begrudge him his pleasure because she knew that he still loved her, even though his love was not a love of the flesh but of the spirit…

The scientists packed their household effects and furniture and this time they paid the movers with their own considerable bank accounts…

The End (no. 1)

Now, for those of you who like "happy ends," let me roll back the time to a point before Armand perpetrated his crime!

Chapter 21:
Donner and Axel rejoice and thank God and the scientists

The two scientists, Jim and Armand prepared the intended conversion suspension with Carbon nanotubes, the replicated **heterosexual** DNA fragments, plus, of course, the Cambridge CRISPR. The heterosexual DNA fragments were synthesized in DNA synthesizer and multiplied by a PCR process with starters and enders, but without a fluorescent stain.

The three necessary ingredients were suspended in a physiological salt solution like the one given to patients suffering from extreme sunburn and dehydration in a hospital.

The two scientists, Jim, and Armand also prepared a control suspension that consisted only of Carbon nanotubes suspended in physiological salt solution. The scientists decided to leave the 2 suspensions for 24 hours at room temperature to complete the absorption of the active ingredients. Night came, and Jim, who was exhausted from the eventful and emotional day left home.

Armand stayed some more to watch the suspensions and to ascertain that both the loaded and the control suspensions will not undergo a process of aggregation into large lumps. He, therefore, shook the two suspensions every quarter of an hour for 2 hours.

Finally, feeling certain that the suspensions are behaving well he left for home.

The next day, early in the morning, the 6 Evangelist subjects, wearing the blood-pressure measuring instruments on their private members, were invited to watch pornographic movies to establish a control line.

The penile blood pressure readings of all gay people threatened to run off the scale during the control screening and satisfied the scientists, and even the strictest scientist, Jim.

Then, the first trio of gay people were ushered in and June, with a steady hand, and with a syringe with a long needle injected the men, with 2 milliliters of the correction suspension.

Then the second control trio of gay people was also ushered in, and they were injected with 2 milliliters of the loaded carbon nanotubes. The 2 gay trios were invited to wait in the dining hall where they were fed with Perl cooking. In the meantime, the nervous scientists gathered in the conference room to wait impatiently and to give vent to their worries and excitement. They knew that they are on the verge of either a resounding victory, or a dismal defeat… Perl offered them also lunch that they barely ate and just fiddled with it without any appetite.

Finally, at 4 o'clock, which was arbitrarily set as the cut-off time arrived, and the scientists invited the gay people to watch again the pornographic gay movies in trios.

The first trio, which consisted of control men injected with a placebo suspension, was invited first to watch the movies… to cut a long story short, the control trio enjoyed the movies and their blood pressures reacted by rocketing off the scale

The trio of gay people who were injected with the correction suspension reacted erratically in the 'porno watching session' and their peaks of penile excitement reached about a quarter of the length of the scale. The scientists told all the test subjects to return to their hotel, order meals by room service, not to leave their rooms, and be ready for a repeat performance of the porno tests on the next morning.

The scientists sat down to discuss the results. They were disappointed that the recording needle moved at all, but all of them were pleased with the promising results.

Next morning the gay people were tested again. The trio injected with the control suspension showed the same behavior as yesterday. But the other trio showed a flat line near the bottom of the scale, and with only occasional small peaks every several minutes.

The scientists celebrated the results with their victory-applause and dances. Professor Hunter went to inform Donner and Axel who was home because of the summer vacation.

When the professor told Donner the happy results on the videophone, he was surprised at Donner's reaction – the serious and calm billionaire uttered a series of Indian yells plus what could only interpreted as dance steps! Axel followed suite and both kneeled and said a prayer of thanks to God.

Professor Hunter laughed and for a moment thought to imitate Donner and Axel but refrained, because of his age and the presence of his colleagues. The professor also suggested an explanation of the small peaks in the recording. He reminded his team that even straight men may get slightly excited on watching deviant pornographic films…

The professor told his teammates to open the champagne bottles that were cooling for eons in Perl's refrigerators. professor Hunter said that the work with his scientists in the final years of his career, was very uplifting and something that he never expected to happen.

Then he said: "we did our best and this bore fruit. I spoke with Donner, and he is very satisfied! All his targets bore fruit. He was happy with the fact that Axel will soon, in a few days, become a heterosexual, and that he may have one grandson or more who will be corrected to permanent heterosexuality while still a fetus!

The professor said that Donner assigned to each of them a "measly" severance-pay of 7 million dollars and asked that the 2 molecular geneticists, Armand, and Jim and Jill be available for the corrective treatment of the fetus when the time will come.

A lot of money remained in start-up's Bank Deposit after all the deduction of all the expenses. The happy Donner told Hunter to transfer all the remaining money to Hunter's private account and it must be said that this was not a measly sum. The grateful professor thanked Donner and told him that when he started his scientific career, he never thought, even in his wildest dreams, that it will make him into a millionaire. The most that he ever hoped was to earn a Nobel prize with its "measly" million and some dollars… Donner was happy at Hunter's reaction and both men swore everlasting friendship…

Two special deep freezers were assigned for the corrected DNA fragments and the Cambridge CRISPR. They were stored in the Psychology department and were cared by a dependable well-compensated member of the department.

The final meeting was very emotional with the post-docs happy about the sudden riches that they received, and sad that they will have to depart from dear friends and colleagues, and from their Boss and mentor who is going to start a "career" of fishing and golf…

The professor and June said goodbye privately in June's apartment… They understood that an enjoyable interlude in their lives ended because the professor will not have an excuse to stay away nights from home. Besides, June wanted to continue her scientific career and was looking forward to new adventures with "mature men"… Several years later, Flora admitted that she knew that her husband had an extramarital affair but did not begrudge him his pleasure, because she knew that he still loved her, even though it was not a love of the flesh but of the spirit…

The scientists packed their household effects and furniture and this time they paid for the movers with their own considerable fortune!

The End (no. 2)

THE AUTHORS BIOGRAPHY

The author obtained an M. Sc. Degree in Microbiology from the University of Tel-Aviv and a Ph.D. degree in virology from the university of Pennsylvania's Medical School.

Later he worked several years at the Virology institute of the St. louis University and then moved to the pharmaceutical Industry in Israel.

He has always been interested in Science-Fiction and had published three SF novels.

He is retired now and lives in Tel-Aviv. He is married, has two sons, two daughters-in-law and three grandsons

Printed by Libri Plureos GmbH in Hamburg, Germany